Per Gunnar Evander

Twayne's World Authors Series

Leif Sjoberg, Editor of Swedish Literature

State University of New York at Stony Brook

TWAS 650

PER GUNNAR EVANDER
Photograph by Bengt Åke Kimbré

Per Gunnar Evander

By Karin Petherick

University College, London

Twayne Publishers • *Boston*

Per Gunnar Evander

Karin Petherick

Copyright © 1982
Twayne Publishers
A Division of G. K. Hall & Company
70 Lincoln Street
Boston, Massachusetts 02111

Printed on permanent/durable acid-free
paper and bound in The United States of
America

Library of Congress Cataloging in Publication Data

Petherick, Karin, 1929-
  Per Gunnar Evander.

  (Twayne's world authors series; TWAS 650)
  Bibliography: p. 139
  Includes index.
  1. Evander, Per Gunnar, 1933-   .—Criticism
and interpretation. I. Title. II. Series.
PT9876.15.V3Z83   839.7'87409   81-6953
ISBN 0-8057-6493-3   AACR2

For Rupert with love

Contents

About the Author

Karin Petherick teaches Swedish literature at University College, London. She received her doctorate from the University of Uppsala on a dissertation about style imitation in three novels by the Swedish writer Hjalmar Bergman. Her particular interests lie in the field of textual analysis and narratology. She has written articles on the novels of a number of Swedish authors. She is currently collaborating with Professor Göran Stockenström of the University of Minnesota on an annotated translation into English of the whole of Strindberg's *Occult Diary*.

Preface

There is a popular conception of Swedishness as quintessentially lonely, guilt-ridden, and afflicted by an indefinable melancholy—a view fostered by the films of Ingmar Bergman. Per Gunnar Evander's intense love of the silent, sparsely populated landscape of his home province of Gästrikland, the emotional reserve of his fictional characters, and the difficulty they encounter in communicating with each other, the nameless fear which afflicts many of them, all fit in with this picture. In an important respect, however, Evander goes counter to another view of Swedes, namely, that they, comfortably neutral and free of colonial guilt, tend to arrogate to themselves the task of being the consciences of the West—a national characteristic neatly defined by an American character in a novel by P. O. Enquist with the words, "The Swedes have the world's only transportable consciences; they go around like professional moralists."[1] Evander's work, on the contrary, shows him to be a man who recognizes that he need only look within himself and at the plight of his fellow citizens, whether they be working on a slippery tin roof, in a dusty brickworks, or in a damp storeroom, to realize the need for active humanity. He does not seek to expiate guilt in far off places. Indeed, his novel *The Physics Master's Sorrowful Eyes* is about a man who observes and classifies phenomena in the distant skies, but is unable—with tragic consequences—to solve his own immediate problems and fulfill his obligations to those closest to him.

No full-length study of Evander's work has yet been published in Sweden, although he has been the subject of numerous articles, and I gratefully acknowledge the seminal essay on him by Matts Rying on which I have drawn freely.[2] The present monograph represents the overdue, first detailed investigation of his work in any language. His achievements and output are of a quality and importance eminently deserving attention. He has yet to be translated into English, and I hope this study may serve to introduce an author whose overriding preoccupation is to help—through his books and plays—toward the building of a more humane society. In that sense his works can be said to be performative—to appropriate J. L. Austin's term—as well as narrative. His powerful and original talent has continuously, in a climate (as we shall see) inimical to personal and existential concerns, found new ways of presenting the individual, that basic unit, source, and instrument of all our knowledge about ourselves and the world.

In preparing this study I have had the pleasure of many conversations with Per Gunnar Evander, and I owe him a great debt of gratitude for his patience and cooperation. I have indicated in notes when statements of fact in this book derive from my conversations with him. My personal opinions, however, I naturally do not ascribe to him, least of all my interpretations of his novels, since I believe there is widespread agreement that once a writer has penned the last word of a work of literature, he has completed *his* task.

The chronology sets out significant milestones in Evander's life. The biographical chapter attempts to present the background against which he grew into a writer. The following three chapters offer a critical-analytical assessment of his books in chronological order, which inevitably means that the first of these chapters deals with works which show us an author learning his craft. Next comes a chapter devoted to his radio and stage plays and television films, and finally there is an evaluation of his work as a whole.

I have throughout my text used English translations of the titles of Evander's works, occasionally in self-explanatory abbreviated forms, e.g., *Foreman Lundin* for *Foreman Lundin of the Brickworks and the Wide World*. The Swedish titles will be found in the bibliography. Quotations from his works are followed by page references to first editions. All translations from his works are my own.

I should like to record my gratitude to the Swedish Institute for accommodation in the Strindberg Museum, Stockholm, in September 1977, and to the Central Research Fund of the University of London, which kindly gave a travel grant on the same occasion. I am also immensely grateful to Professor Peter Foote of University College London for reading my manuscript, for his many valuable suggestions, and for his invariable kindness and encouragement. I should like to thank Sheila Rust for typing part of the manuscript for me. I am much indebted to Per Gunnar Evander's wife Agneta Brunius, to his mother Mrs. Roddie Evander, to Olle Westin, Göran Norström, and to Carl Olof Lång for kindly agreeing to talk to me, as I am to my friends Kerstin Berglund and Ingegerd Jörtsö for making my stay in Sandviken so pleasant. Finally, treating first things last, my profound thanks go to Professor Leif Sjöberg, the editor of the Scandinavian Series of the Twayne World Authors, for giving me the opportunity of writing this study, for his wise and helpful advice which has been of inestimable value, and for his inspiring devotion to Swedish literature.

Karin Petherick

University College, London

Chronology

1933   Per Gunnar Evander born 25 April 1933 in Ovansjö near Sandviken, two hundred miles northwest of Stockholm.

1949   Works as lumberjack during summer vacation. Starts serious physical training (mainly running), participates in sports camp for "Tomorrow's Champions" (*Morgondagens män*).

1954   Matriculates from Sandviken High School.

1954–1955   National service.

1955   Casual labor, including rolling-mill work at Sandviken Ironworks and employment at local brickworks.

1956   Attends training college for elementary school teachers in Gävle.

1957   First short story published in newspaper *Gefle Dagblad*. Vacation work as auxiliary at mental hospital.

1958   Wins short-story competition for Scandinavian teacher training colleges. Graduates from training college and teaches physics and math at elementary school in Storvik, near Sandviken. Starts reviewing books in *Gefle Dagblad*. First journey abroad: London.

1959   Summer vacation in Spain.

1960   Leaves teaching job in Storvik and embarks on academic studies at Uppsala University. Continues as reviewer in *Gefle Dagblad* (mainly modern poetry).

1963   Graduates in comparative literature and economic history from Uppsala University. Takes up position as teacher at Gästrikland's folk high school.

1965   First novel *Close Relations*. Moves to Wik's folk high school, south-southwest of Uppsala.

1966   First radio play *It's Sunday afternoon and my brother's running across the field* broadcast and published. Four more radio plays broadcast. Accepts offer of job as dramaturge by the Swedish Broadcasting Corporation and moves to Stockholm.

1967   *Dear Mr. Evander* (novel). Two more radio plays broadcast, and one of them, *The Wild Strawberry Troll*, published. Offered permanent job by the Swedish Broadcasting Corporation.

1968   Starts as producer of radio plays. *The Physics Master's Sorrowful Eyes* (novel) and *As day grows cool* (radio play). Moves to TV section of Swedish Broadcasting Corporation and attends TV producers' course.

1969   *The Upstarts—An Investigation* (novel), awarded the Literary Prize for 1969 by *Svenska Dagbladet*. *The Demonstrator* (radio play). Gävleborg County's Arts Prize. Own TV programs screened for the first time.

1970   Father dies. *Foreman Lundin of the Brickworks and the Wide World* (novel) and *In my youth I often looked at myself in the mirror* (radio play).

1971   *The Last Day of Valle Hedman's Life* and *A Love Story* (novels) and *My dad also had a silver cup* (radio play). TV films include *Nothing special happened to me in Puerto*, which is voted best TV production of the year. Major scholarship from the Swedish Authors' Association.

1972   Numerous TV programs including films *Per Nilsson was my name* and *The Journey to Strangers Haven*. *The Story of Joseph* (novel) awarded the Swedish Academy's Zorn Prize. Premiere of play *All the days of my life* at Gothenburg City Theater.

1973   *The Last Adventure* (novel) and *It's already dark, it's time to wake Horst Müller* (radio play). Severe autumn depression.

1974   Premiere of film of *The Last Adventure* (directed by Jan Halldoff). *Mondays with Fanny* (novel). Paperback edition of *The Upstarts*. Swedish T.U.C. scholarship for the arts.

1975   *Mondays with Fanny* awarded the Major Prize of the Society for the Promotion of Literature. Premiere of *The Goldfish* performed by Uppsala City Theater in Sandviken; also performed at Gothenburg City Theater and Malmö City Theater. *All the days of my life* revived at Royal Dramatic Theater, Stockholm. *Earth Divine* (novel) published as Book of the Month. Paperback editions of *Foreman Lundin* and *The Last Day of Valle Hedman's Life*. Spends six weeks in the United States at invitation of American embassy in Stockholm.

1976   *The Return* (TV film). *Notes from an Uncomfortable Private Life* published. *Two Comedies* (*All the days of my life* and *The Goldfish*). Paperback editions of *The Story of Joseph* and *Mondays with Fanny*; second paperback edition of *The Last Adventure*.

1977   January, *The Snail* (novel) by Lillemor Holm (pseudonym). August, *The Case of Lillemor Holm* (novel). Premiere of film of *Mondays with Fanny* (directed by Bengt Forslund). New editions of *Earth Divine* and *The Last Day of Valle Hedman's Life*. Marries Agneta Brunius.

1978   *Judas Iscariot's Clenched Fists* (novel). *Cheating* (TV film).

1979   *That poor wretch Waldemar* (TV film, screened 1980). Birth of daughter Andrea. New paperback edition of *The Case of Lillemor Holm*.

1980   *See me in My Unblemished Eye* and *Fear's Dwelling Place* (novels).

Chapter One

Introduction and Background

Anecdotary preamble

A young man flees down five flights of stairs in a student-nurses' residence stark naked, clutching his clothes, while a girl's voice floats down the stairwell saying that she was only joking (the electrifying jest was that they were expecting a baby).[1] Another young man, traveling by rail to visit his brother, is informed during the journey that the train does not stop at the desired small country station. He immediately tells the conductor that in that case he will pull the emergency brake. The conductor relents sufficiently to inform him that the train will actually slow down when passing through the station in order for the guard to throw off a small parcel, and he advises the impatient traveler to go to the back of the train, jump off as it slows down, and then run along the platform in the same direction as the train. The young man does this, but makes the mistake of jumping off just before the train has slowed down maximally, and as he runs along the platform and reaches the carriage ahead of his, a hearty gym teacher used to making snap decisions swings open his door, hauls in the running figure, and exclaims: "You sure are in luck—this train doesn't stop here!"[2]

Both anecdotes appear in novels by Evander—and he tells them most engagingly as a public speaker. We must assume that they are apocryphal, but they nonetheless throw light on the complex subject of this monograph. The naked young man fleeing from the weight of human relationships is representative of the many fugitives in Evander's early fiction, and—we venture to suggest—figuratively speaking of the author himself as a young man. The general picture of him at this time was of a solitary—it was known that he lived on his own in a one-room apartment—writing about hunted men.[3] Although his

1

good looks and personal charm suggest that there must have been people willing to share his loneliness, it was not until 1977 that this "eternal bachelor"[4] married a colleague at Swedish Television. His works demonstrate a noticeable progression from detached, behavioristic recording of frightened and lonely people on the run to the presentation of healing processes leading to fulfillment and sociality. It would seem that this is also the general direction of his own inner development.

Anyone meeting Per Gunnar Evander must be struck by his unpretentious friendliness and ready humor. Yet these precise qualities create an effective distance between his interlocutor and his private world. No one could be more helpful and at the same time more elusive. It is hard to escape the conviction that he is a deeply instinctive writer whose works reveal what he cannot and will not verbalize except through the medium of art. Writing this biographical chapter is like playing the role of the officious fellow traveler who hauled the escaping passenger back onto the train. The spirit got away, leaving the traveler clutching his outer covering (context and background). Yet this may serve an introductory purpose. It is in his texts—to which our remaining chapters are devoted—that we really get to know him.

The anxiety of the middle-distance runner

The above travesty of Alan Sillitoe's novel title seems peculiarly apt when applied to Evander. He grew up with a strong sense of emotional loneliness, which is reflected in the characters his fiction portrays, and for a number of adolescent years he trained conscientiously as a runner and studied every move of his idol, the Swedish champion Gunder Hägg. He never achieved his ambitions as a middle-distance runner, but the obsessive nature of his ambition, his will to power, seem rooted in profound feelings of insecurity. He still retains his passionate interest in sport and never misses an important ice hockey or football match.

When Evander was invited to contribute a self-portrait to a magazine, he chose to highlight two contrasting incidents from his boyhood when he dreamed of becoming a successful sportsman.[5] In the one, a discus thrower needlessly tramples on the boy's frail self-confidence; in the other, a football coach tells him that the most important thing in the game, as in life, is having the right contact with your fellow players, knowing the exact and fruitful distance to keep, the distance which is right for you personally. As he puts it, looking back:

> To find one's own "distance" in life!
> That really would be to be in control of the game with fellow players and ɔpponents in the surrounding world!
> That would be never to lose contact in either attack or defense, never to be inveigled into fruitless attempts at solo performances![6]

It is typical that the nonsmoking, well-trained ex-athlete Evander should find his metaphors in the field of sport. It is also characteristic that despite his respect for physical toughness and training, he does not favor the stiff-upper-lip stance. On the contrary, his later works demonstrate how important it is to release your pain. In this same self-portrait he writes openly of sleeplessness, exhaustion, and despair, of lying curled up in bed, firmly determined never to get up again. The poles of hope and despair are symbolized by the two sportsmen he places at the center of his recollections, the one discouraging, the other encouraging the young boy. In numerous novels and plays, Evander shows us people who have never received the encouragement necessary for full personal development. He feels strongly that too many small children are not treated with the consideration due to them, and quotes the French doctor Frédéric Leboyer who stresses the vital importance of the actual moment of birth and the reception accorded to the newborn babe.[7] He is appalled that there are parents who beat their children, just as he deplores the psychological cruelty many children are subjected to by their parents. But parents were once children themselves, and he can write of parental-filial relationships with compassion for both parties.

The family

Per Gunnar Evander was born on 25 April 1933 near the small industrial town of Sandviken, where his father was a clerk in the foreign department of Sandvikens Jernverk ironworks. Since both his father and the ironworks played a decisive part in young Per Gunnar's development, they are worth dwelling on.

The Evander family had its roots in Skåne in the south of Sweden, where most of its members were modest farmers and smallholders. In the middle of the nineteenth century, Per Gunnar's great-grandfather studied theology and in the fullness of time he became a respected minister in the Church of Sweden. One of his sons in turn became a minister, one of his daughters studied medicine, and another son—Per Gunnar's grandfather—became an army officer. This same army captain died young, leaving his widow in the old university town of Lund to bring up two small sons on a meager pension. The elder of the two, Per, was to become Per Gunnar's father. A clergyman uncle offered to finance his theological studies, but he refused the offer on principle, since he was an agnostic. Instead, he successfully completed a first-year university course in English, earning his keep meanwhile, but lacked the financial means to continue, and was unwilling—again on principle—to borrow money. So he accepted sponsored training at a commercial college and subsequently worked for a Swedish firm in Germany for eight years, until his return to Sweden in 1933 and his new employment at Sandviken. He can be seen as a man disappointed in his academic ambitions but proud of his principles, whose daytime employment as a clerk dealing with foreign correspondence was augmented by the role of foreign language teacher at evening classes. Indeed, his son came to regard him as a "typical schoolmaster," whose devotion to the correct use of Swedish is remembered both by youthful visitors to the Evander home, who had their grammatical slips corrected, and by colleagues at work, who recall the zeal with which he collected linguistic solecisms from press and radio.[8] He was a pedantic, deeply conservative man with unshakeable middle-class loyalties, who came to spend most of his working life (he died in 1970) in an industrial town with a rigidly hierarchical class structure. His wife Linnea, who also grew up in Lund, came from a different social background, her father being a carpenter and socialist trade unionist, active in local government. Their son Per Gunnar describes them as being "highly incompatible,"[9] and as a child he found their quarrels frightening. He recollects his sister, four years his senior, being brought up with extreme harshness. With her example before his eyes, he became a compliant and meek child, lacking a sense of being warmly and securely accepted, with consequent grave long-term emotional effects. Exploring the relationships between parents and children was later to become one of the central concerns of his literary work.

Sandviken

There is something special about growing up in a works town like Sandviken. In 1862 C. F. Göransson pioneered Bessemer steel and founded his ironworks among the forests of Gästrikland by a sandy bay of Lake Storsjön. Now his creation has grown into an industry employing well over 10,000 people in Sandviken alone and with over thirty subsidiary companies elsewhere. In a real sense the works *are* the town, they are its origin and its lifeblood. Broadly speaking, the inhabitants of Sandviken all have some sort of connection with the works and fit into the categories of management, clerical staff, or workers. The psychological effect of this stratification is much like that obtaining in a military or educational establishment—people know their place. An unwritten Sandviken law decrees: Thou shalt not presume. Thou shalt observe thy station.

Apart from manufacturing high quality steel products, there is another activity in which Sandvikers excel—interestingly enough also a collective one—namely, sport, in particular football and ice hockey. This interest in sport is known from other Swedish works communities and is explained by the fact that steady local employment means a continuous flow of young players, for whom the works traditionally provide facilities. High prestige attaches to athletic prowess in Sandviken, and to the virtues associated with it—endurance and stoicism, most commonly coupled to verbal reticence. Any reader of Evander's books is struck by the number of references to sporting ambitions and achievements, often in connection with the first-person narrator. Clearly, the Sandviken view of sport as an unassailably legitimate endeavor, a way of proving oneself as a man, has left deep marks on him. While still a youngster, he was picked out as a potential running ace for participation in a sports camp for "Tomorrow's Champions." The fact that he failed to live up to the selectors' expectations can only have increased his sense of personal failure and reinforced his need to redouble his efforts to prove himself, perhaps also in some other field. Literary and intellectual aspirations were, however, regarded with skepticism in his home town. Sandviken had no traditions of that kind. The town's one established literary figure was the poet Stig Sjödin (b. 1917) who had worked in the iron foundry before becoming a writer. It was reading his poems which first showed the adolescent Evander that "poetry is not necessarily a Sunday pastime."[10] Here was a poet whose social observation was as incisive as his aesthetic achievement was impressive. Some years later Evander was to write an undergraduate dissertation on Sjödin's collection *Sotfragment* [Fragments of Soot] in which the cycle *Porträtt från bruket* [Portraits from the Works] captures in lapidary style the moods and conditions of the foundry workers. Both men knew what it was to grow up in a town where all really important emotions remain unspoken. For the poet, the people's silence was charged with a meaning communicable by metaphor. As for Evander, the isolation experienced in both forest and town by people who chose "rather to be silent than speak a superfluous word," drove him to explore communication in the form of novels and plays.[11]

The underdog

Most of Evander's schoolmates came from working-class homes, and the only vacation jobs available to teenagers in Sandviken were manual ones. So he felled timber and worked in the foundry. He experienced unremitting physical labor. These friendships and experiences were good reasons for solidarity with the workers (as was his reaction against the compact conservatism of his home). Yet without wishing to detract from his genuine socialist concern for the underprivileged, it is tempting to see his identification with them as also being the fruit of his own private sense of vulnerability and disadvantage. He has described his youth as "one long humiliation," with "dreams and hopes being continuously crushed. One was never allowed to count for anything . . . was never allowed to assert oneself. One just had to swallow injustices."[12] Added to which came the taboo on voicing one's pain: "I belonged to a generation which was brought up not to show any emotions or gentle feelings."[13] One's real self was invisible—and the invisibility of the underdog is a recurrent theme in his work, often developed with great effectiveness and ingenuity in his radio plays. It may interest American readers to know that when asked by the author of the present monograph if Ralph Ellison's novel *Invisible Man* (1963) had stimulated him, Evander wrote back that he had never heard of Ellison, and continued: "Invisibility is a long-standing theme in my work, particularly as regards my plays. Scarcely being visible or not being visible at all is only a slight extension of the sense of inferiority and lack of self-confidence which I so frequently and readily dwell upon."[14]

His personal choice of a short story for a series run by a big daily paper reinforces his point. It was a story by the Swedish writer Stig Dagerman (1923-54), and he explains in his introductory commentary that when he first read it at the age of fifteen, he suddenly recognized *his own situation* in a literary text for the first time in his life. Three barefoot children on a small farm, wearing outgrown clothes, struggling with endless manual tasks, feeling clumsy and ignorant, meet a shining car with a Stockholm number plate as they chase cows home along a lane. They have never seen anything so beautiful as the car, in the back seat of which sits a little girl of their own age in a white hat. But neither the driver, who gets out to inspect a scratch on the car from a cow's horn, nor the little girl, bestow as much as a glance upon them. "We were afraid of getting a hiding, now as always, but that was not what we were most afraid of. What we feared most was something else, that the Stockholmer would not say a single word to us, that we simply would not exist."[15] Why, we may ask ourselves, should the teenage Evander identify so strongly with these children? Perhaps because in the story the rural poor function as a symbol and metaphor for humiliation and shame.

Friendships

Three men befriended and encouraged the young Evander in his home town, "people who gave injections."[16] They were the amateur actor and producer Olle Westin ("my life's first real artist"), who gave him a chance to develop his interest in the theater; the journalist Sven-Åke Dahlbäck, whose warm-hearted socialism strengthened his political sympathies; and the teacher and philosopher Johan Nygren, who had in the past acted as Socratic mentor to no less a person than the legendary Stig Dagerman himself. Evander went regularly to Dahlbäck's home to hear Nygren hold forth on a variety of topics. It is symptomatic of the spirit of free inquiry at these meetings and the youthful audience's opposition to Sandviken's hierarchical social order, that two of the four youngsters became painters, and two—Evander and his friend Göran Norström—writers.

Göran Norström's father, like Evander's, was a clerk at the ironworks, and both youngsters were subject to the conformist pressures of their hometown. But the resemblance goes deeper. Norström has never made a secret of his acute anxiety symptoms, and a number of his books deal directly with people struggling with emotional problems and mental illness. Norström and Evander also have a certain physical resemblance. When the author Evander has dealt with anxiety states and hypochondria, he has—as it were—had an objective correlative in the person of Norström, which has enabled him to treat painful *personal* experiences at one remove. Their friendship has lasted through the years, and Evander returns to Gästrikland, to his mother and the Norström family, when he needs to get away from the pressure of life in Stockholm. His love of nature is intense and Norström has recollections of Evander getting up at dawn and returning from two-hour runs through the forest in time for breakfast.[17]

The long road to self-expression

Evander wrote in his schoolboy diary that he wanted to become a theatrical producer or writer, being already at this stage an avid consumer of radio drama. The encouragement he derived from joining Olle Westin's amateur theatrical society helped him immeasurably in his struggle for self-expression, but his deep-seated lack of self-confidence put a brake on his ability to exploit his creative talent successfully. He was altogether a slow starter, failing to be moved up a grade at school once and matriculating on the eve of his twenty-first birthday. Coming out of the army after national service, he embarked on university studies in Uppsala but soon abandoned them and returned to Sandviken with a wretched sense of failure. Years later, he was to write of his alter ego, his (nonexistent) brother, at the same stage of life: "While Henning drifted around as a loner . . . most of his friends became active in political movements and organizations which propelled them into the mainstream of life. He himself was caught in a reflex which all the time forced him back and out into the periphery of society, forced him to stare down into himself and seek protection against the surrounding world instead of participating in it, a surrounding world which came to appear more and more menacing and whose only accepted representatives were distant and ruthless powers in the shape of the police, the army, and the moneyed ruling class."[18] For over a year Evander was employed as a laborer at the local ironworks and brickworks. As was to be expected, his parents were concerned at their son's apparent lack of ambition and success and were greatly relieved when he subsequently in 1956 got a place at the Teacher Training College in Gävle. At this stage his specialization was science-based, and when he graduated as a teacher in 1958, he went to teach physics and math at Storvik Elementary School near Sandviken. By now he was reviewing books for the paper *Gefle Dagblad* and publishing occasional short stories and prose pieces. After two years as a teacher, he returned to Uppsala University, this time concentrating on the humanities and reading for a degree in economic history and comparative literature. His studies were successful, but he recalls himself as being exceedingly shy and far too diffident to join any literary coterie.

Evander graduated from Uppsala in 1963 at the age of thirty, and went to teach at Västerberg's folk high school near Sandviken. A folk high school is a typically Swedish (and Scandinavian) educational establishment offering residential courses on a variety of subjects to all types and ages of student. Two years later, in 1965, he published his first book, *Close Relations*, and moved to Wik's folk high school near Uppsala. Shortly thereafter, he wrote his first radio play, which was enthusiastically received by the Swedish Broadcasting Corporation. Spurred on, he wrote four more radio plays in quick succession and in 1966 the Corporation offered him a job as resident dramatist. In 1968 he moved across to Swedish Television and trained as a producer and filmmaker. This is still at the time of writing his permanent full-time employment.

Evander possesses an immense capacity for hard work. His output has been prolific once he got started—roughly a novel each year, flanked by plays for radio, stage, and television. For the past decade his creative work (as opposed to routine employment) has alternated between the lonely pursuit of writing and the social activity of making television films, and he has said of himself that he is a happy person when making a film and "an extremely unhappy person" when writing.[19] We must suppose that without the relief supplied by spells of teamwork, he could not endure the strain of writing novels dealing directly with painful and explosive personal issues.

The writer and his literary background

As a young man, Evander felt a "boundless" admiration for Hemingway; looking back, he thinks it must have been the sentimentality under the hard-boiled surface, the combination of toughness and emotion, which attracted him.[20] The Swedish novelist P. O. Sundman (b. 1922), a master of the detached, behavioristic mode, is another author to whom he professes great indebtedness; indeed, he uses the metaphor of Sundman being responsible for his "delivery" (in the obstetric sense) as a writer.[21] Kafka was in on the birth too, as Evander's first two books demonstrate. In 1965 he ran a summer course on Kafka at his folk high school, rejoicing in the precise realism which merges into unreality. "Kafka has taught me a lot when it comes to describing pathological states,"[22] he recalls. We shall also see that Strindberg the dramatist inspired the playwright Evander, and that Pär Lagerkvist (1891–1974) meant a lot to the short-story writer. In spite of this, Evander claims never to have been a voracious devourer of books; life—including sport—has always seemed to him quite as interesting as literature.[23]

In a Swedish context the decade in which Evander reached adulthood, the 1950s, was labeled a time of pluralism or relativism.[24] Reacting against the polarizations of the Cold War, the poet and journalist Karl Vennberg (b. 1910) coined the phrase "the third standpoint" (*tredje ståndpunkten*), which stood for nonalignment. Perhaps the most striking thing about the 1950s was the widely prevalent conviction that an individually achieved truth was the best alternative to group ideologies, powerfully expressed in their different ways by Pär Lagerkvist and Lars Gyllensten (b. 1921). Lagerkvist's Nobel Prize winning novel *Barabbas* (1950) and his subsequent five novels were studies in lonely individuals seeking a personal salvation.[25] Gyllensten represented the skeptic who forswore ideologies: "One of the cornerstones of my work is my aversion to and polemics against the definitive."[26]

But the literary climate was to change in the 1960s in response to a decade which saw the student revolt movement in the United States move swiftly to Europe, which noted the increasing gap between rich and poor nations, and which woke up to the brutality of the war in Vietnam. A seminal article—"Are we being had?"[27]—in the evening paper *Expressen* in 1965 questioned standard assumptions about the unassailable morality of Western democracy and capitalism, which overtly or tacitly had underpinned Swedish political thinking up to that time. Its author, Göran Palm, went on to write *En orättvis betraktelse* [An unfair view, 1966], in which he attempts to see Western Europe through Third World eyes, and he then topped this with the polemical book *Indoktrineringen i Sverige* [Indoctrination in Sweden, 1968], which sets out to demonstrate the countless ways Swedes are unconsciously and subliminally affected by values and standards which on closer inspection turn out to be undesirable. The raising of people's level of political awareness—what South Americans call *Conscienciatizacion*[28] and Swedes *att medvetandegöra*—became a vital aim. In 1970 Palm signed on anonymously as a worker with the L. M. Ericsson Telephone Co., subsequently writing a book challenging the concern's power structure and its authoritarian form of staff communications. Naturally, he did not inaugurate a mood of critical inquiry and sociopolitical involvement all by himself, but he will serve here as a paradigm of its exponents, for—as a colleague of his put it— Göran Palm is so Swedish that he could be exhibited at Skansen (Stockholm's Open Air Museum).[29]

Other writers increased their political awareness by visits to India and China (Sven Lindqvist and Jan Myrdal) or gave up writing novels altogether in favor of political journalism and documentaries (Sara Lidman). The justification for the novel as a literary form had become problematic to a number of its practitioners, since a purely imaginative approach to writing risked appearing frivolous in a world which required hard thinking about unpalatable facts. The documentary novel seemed to offer an acceptable alternative to the traditional narrative approach, and the genre became productive in Sweden, the internationally best-known titles being P. O. Enquist's *The Legion-*

naires and P. O. Sundman's *The Flight of the "Eagle."*[30] It was against this background—the shift from the lively interest in formal aesthetics and existentialism which had characterized the 1950s and early 1960s to the earnest social commitment of the ensuing Vietnam decade—that Evander published his early works. In 1965 he sent in a batch of poems and a prose work to the publishers Bonniers, who accepted the prose for publication under the title *Close Relations,* thereby helping him to choose his future medium—prose rather than poetry.

In order to appreciate Evander's subsequent situation as a writer we must remember that for the next fifteen years a highly articulate Marxist lobby propounded a radical orthodoxy which saw literature as an instrument of sociopolitical struggle and condemned subjective and personal novels as reactionary, individualistic, and/or naive. A retrospective summation of the situation of Swedish literature during the late 1960s, written by a Marxist critic, puts their case succinctly: "At the same time as new literary modes developed, the author's traditional role was subjected to radical rethinking. . . . The documentary and factual style accorded pride of place to the message to be communicated, and relegated the individual author to a more inconspicuous plane than before . . . . The author's task was no longer to express his or her personality and experiences, but rather to act as a channel for his or her factual knowledge . . . . There was no real scope for the free play of imagination and invention any longer . . . immediate reality ought to constitute a sufficient basis for writing."[31] The opening pages of Evander's novel *A Love Story* (1971) illustrates these pressures nicely, with the narrator wrestling with his—ultimately inescapable— urge to write about a personal relationship and speaking of the danger of being "too private or in some other way running the risk of not being universal enough" (9).

Two phases of a public career

Evander's public career as a writer can be roughly divided into two phases. During the first phase he was steadily engaged in building up a reputation. Between 1966 and 1972 his twelve radio plays were performed more abroad than those of any other Swedish radio dramatist.[32] As a novelist, he was recognized as "one of the most exciting resources of Swedish literature in the 1970s"[33] already in the first year of that decade. His critical prestige was high, but his reading public was still limited. He was thought of as a writer with a complex style and exclusive appeal.

It seemed vitally important to Evander to reach out to a wider audience. Just as a distinguished Swedish predecessor Hjalmar Bergman (1883–1931) had been considered "difficult" and even depressing until he deliberately, by a stroke of creative genius, succeeded in finding a form for his novel *Markurells i Wadköping* [God's Orchid, 1919][34] which delighted the broad reading public by its humor while yet at a deeper level retaining the urgency of his serious message, so in 1973 Evander transformed himself from a writer Swedes had heard of but only a minority had read, into a best-selling novelist with his moving and funny account of a young man's tribulations in *The Last Adventure* (filmed the following year). He kept up his success with *Mondays with Fanny* (1974), also filmed, and *Earth Divine* (1975). Interest was stirred in his earlier works, which were reprinted in paperback editions. His first stage play, *All the days of my life*, was first performed in 1972, and 1975 saw its revival as well as the premiere of his second play *The Goldfish*, so that he was played at a total of five theaters that year.

Suddenly Evander had become tremendously successful. We shall see in chapter 4 that in 1975 a large daily paper devoted considerable space to reporting a critics symposium held to discuss his novel *Earth Divine*. The ten participants held differing views on the book's merits, but were generally agreed that Evander ought to "spend more time" over his next novel. The object of this sort of attention must feel like a child up before a panel of teachers. Evander is known to be highly sensitive to press criticism. He wrote in 1969 that in one respect being a writer was "strictly speaking Hell," insofar as it involved being at the mercy of "nonchalant, bored, alcoholized, and spiteful critics."[35] At all events, he did not publish his regular autumn book in 1976. Not only did he spend longer on it, he devised a form for it which made *The Case of Lillemor Holm* the literary sensation of 1977, selling over 100,000 copies in the first printing—a lot for Sweden. Let us not at this stage expand on the mystery connected with this book, but merely note that it, like *The Upstarts—An Investigation* (1969), illustrates Evander's quite remarkable gift for fantasy and dissimulation for creative ends. We shall argue in chapter 6 that he belongs to the school of the writer as magician (as opposed to the writer as reporter). For him, writing is an art, not a political or sociological function.

Now, three books later, Evander is in the vanguard of Swedish literature. He has not changed, but the literary climate has. "Imagination, troubled and troubling emotions, myths, and—even—a willingness to take moral risks, are on their way back,"[36] announces the editorial of a literary journal. They have been there all the time in his work.

Chapter Two

Beginnings

Close Relations

The stories in Evander's first book, *Tjocka släkten* [Close Relations, 1965], all have one-word titles designating family status such as "The Mother," "The Twin," "The Daughter," and so on. In a precise and authoritative way situations are set up which somewhere along the line become absurd. There is the young man—"The Son"—who set out to pick cranberries and fell down a deep, disused well. He is trapped at the bottom of the narrow shaft and can only peer upward for a glimpse of the world above. "It won't do you any harm," says his father when he discovers his son twenty-four hours later, adding with a chortle, "we're meant to aim high in life" (93). His mother shows more sympathy, for she "hardly ever laughs" (93), and occasionally surreptitiously lowers him some woollen underpants and jerseys against the cold and damp. He soon loses all sense of time, but there comes a point when he suspects that autumn has come round again, and so, indeed, it must have, for his father returns and bellows to him, "let's have that basket!" (94). Not long afterward some workmen can be heard sawing and hammering, and they fit a lid to the mouth of the well. The young man confirms that they have done a good job, "it had never before been so dark down there." The following day one of the workmen returns and impregnates the lid with a special oil, which fills the well with a pungent smell which takes a long time to disperse.

Everything is observed from the outside. No analysis of motives or states of mind is proferred—these have to be supplied by the reader between the lines. Hemingway and the Swede P. O. Sundman were Evander's models in the art of behavioristic narration. His sharp satirical bite was inspired by Pär Lagerkvist's *Evil Tales*,[1] whose powerful simplicity and logical absurdities are reflected in many of his stories.

The stories are all prefaced by short italicized passages which taken together indicate a group of relations ganging up against and relentlessly hounding an outsider. That these passages are to be read as a parable of inhumanity is clear from the biblical associations aroused when the local policeman tells the gang that they have been hounding a relative and they reply with an obvious paraphrase of St. John 19:20, "Don't say that he is a relation of ours, but say that he claims to be a relation of ours," and the policeman replies in the manner of Pilate, "What I have said, I have said."[2] It was Hemingway's use of italicized prefatory passages in *The First Forty-Nine Stories* which gave Evander the idea, and he uses it skillfully to counterpoint the macrocosmic family setup presented in the italicized passages with the microcosmic or individual situations of the stories. The book is a talented and remarkably assured exercise by a beginner adopting some of the stances of his mentors. It also provided him with a fund of situations on which he was to build many highly successful radio plays in which people jump off trains traveling at high speed, walk on water, and become invisible. In fact, within a year he was established as resident dramatist at the Swedish Broadcasting Corporation.

Dear Mr. Evander

In 1967 came Evander's second book, *Bäste herr Evander* [Dear Mr. Evander], the title of which derives from the fictitious correspondence it presents, purporting to be letters exchanged by the presidium or governing body of a local association and a certain Per Gunnar Henning Evander, registration number 330425775. A Swedish registration number is issued to every inhabitant of the realm and comprises the year, month, and date of birth in that order, plus three final digits, and it constitutes irrefutable evidence of identity. The number quoted above actually is that of the author, and its introduction into the text, followed by the statement "I always speak the truth," is an indicator of the complicated status of the information purveyed in the novel, which consists of the so-called presidium's acknowledgments of and commentaries on reports sent to it by the said Per Gunnar Evander, who is fleeing from unnamed pursuers. Evander's narrative technique, with particular reference to its epistemological aspect—the reliability and type of information conveyed—will be discussed in chapter 6.

All the reports sent in by the fugitive are gratefully received by the presidium, which is at pains to check all trivially verifiable facts appearing in them. What it steadfastly omits to do throughout is in any way whatever to comment on the heart of the matter—their correspondent's fear and his mysterious pursuers. There is a good deal of unintentional humor in the presidium's replies, couched in impeccable official rhetoric. It solemnly describes, for example, the collections for various good causes made at the end of each public reading of the fugitive's latest installment, and the questions, interruptions, and occasional bizarre incidents which enliven the evening's proceedings. The contrast between the bland comments of the collective on the one hand and the fear of the hunted man on the other carries a powerful message of alienation. The presidium makes itself absurd by straining at gnats and swallowing camels, by commending its informant on the accuracy of his data concerning his physical surroundings, and by noting minor divergences of measurement or appearance, while they entirely fail to appreciate his essential predicament. What has happened is that the man has wakened from a light sleep at night and heard "them" whispering outside his house. His pursuers, whose identity remains nebulous, are out to get him, and the woman he lives with is guilty by association with them, he believes. He emotions on seeing her sleeping figure before he climbs out of the cellar window and dashes for the nearby wood are a compound of resentment and outright physical distaste. Pausing in the wood, he concedes that the light may be playing tricks on his eyes and making him imagine he can see his pursuers at a distance, but of the reality of the pursuit he feels no doubt at all. He describes the terrain he covers with convincing exactitude. He is denied help by a farmer who refuses to get involved, shelters in a forest hut where he ends up by knocking a man out in preemptive self-defence, and then, tired and unwilling, has a grotesque sexual encounter with a smelly and insatiable nymphet who has allowed him to take refuge in a warm boiler-house. His concluding letter finds him still in the forest, surrounded by his pursuers, although they steadfastly refuse to reveal themselves. In this extremity he is comforted by a familiar dream, that of walking across an endless and luminous plain with a feeling of indescribable stillness: "I just walked and walked, and it was a very wide plain. Everything was light and

pleasant and indescribably still. And the plain was never-ending"
(172).

There are themes which insistently recur in Evander's works. The
end of *Dear Mr. Evander* provides a significant one, when the state of
tension and fear communicated in the fugitive's letters is at the very
last superseded by a waking dream of walking timelessly across a plain
suffused with light. Evander's novel *The Upstarts* has a variant of the
luminous landscape, and so have a number of others. The peace and
release from suffering come from a resource stored within the
individual which cannot be deliberately tapped but which opens up
involuntarily at moments of acute strain. It is a mystical experience
which fills the individual with a timeless sense of security in the
universe.[3] All immediate objects and surroundings vanish, and what
remains is an inner state. That the hunted man has access, however
rarely, to this fund of peace or salvation is ultimately—it could be
argued—quite as significant as the persecution he experiences, and it is
just as mysterious and seemingly irrational. There are critics who have
suggested that the urbane benevolence of the presidium, who encouraged the fugitive and arranged public readings of his reports while
never understanding the reality of his fear, could well represent
publishers, readers, and critics, who make encouraging noises while
the author sweats it out alone.[4] This need not be a trivializing
interpretation which deprives the book of its "massive air of mystery,"
as another critic has maintained.[5] For whatever allegorical or analogi-
cal interpretation we favor, it still has to accommodate the lonely
human being at its center, whose feelings are inaccessible to rational
analysis.

That the fictive Per Gunnar Evander is a close relation of Kafka's
bank clerk and the surveyor K. is not hard to see, nor that the
absurdity of the presidium and the book's bizarre sexual incidents have
a certain tenuous likeness with the vicissitudes undergone by Kafka's
heroes. At the same time, there is a sense in which the fugitive's
reports are stylized along the lines of the tough, lone hero of a
Western movie, galloping off into the forest with a posse of the
sheriff's men at his heels, although it never comes to a shoot-out. The
latter comparison is based on Evander's admission that he finds the
same carefully restrained and concealed sentimentality in Westerns

that he so admired in Hemingway's hard-boiled stories and in those of his own compatriot P. O. Sundman. Kafka, Hemingway, and Sundman seem to have offered Evander modes for *controlling* his emotional and creative urges. We shall see that the repression of emotion and the dangers of its inevitable, explosive release constitute the psychological mechanism with which Evander is much concerned in the novels following these two initial works. *Close Relations* and *Dear Mr. Evander* are written with amazing virtuosity for a beginner, but their parabolic form was not one that could be fruitfully repeated. The critical approbation which they gained for their author must have encouraged him to tackle his subject in a more realistic way in his next novel.

The Physics Master's Sorrowful Eyes

Fysiklärarens sorgsna ögon [The Physics Master's Sorrowful Eyes, 1968] has a prefatory motto reputedly taken from an essay written by a pupil who has ruminated over the physical location of the human conscience and come to the conclusion that "our conscience is somehow bound up with our eyes. Which is proved when we close our eyes and cry at the same time." The logic of this remark may not be entirely compelling, but it provides a leitmotiv which is echoed in the book's very title, for the eyes of the middle-aged physics master are of continuous significance, in both the literal and the figurative senses. They are so in the literal sense, not only because his favorite pastime is astronomy and scanning the heavens, but also because he suffers from an optical complaint which makes his pupils think he is weeping. The figurative sense is bound up with the fact that he *shuts his eyes* to his own and his son's emotional needs.

The father. The book is so structured that diary entries written by the teacher alternate by chapter with his seventeen-year-old son's account of life at a folk high school. The fifty-one-year-old physics master is a pedant who says of himself: "I am outwardly even-tempered because I consciously and consistently check every sign of anger or irritation which I occasionally notice in myself" (25). But by the end of the book his repressed emotions erupt into an act of violence, foreshadowed in the diary by mention of the classic symptom of repression—extreme tiredness. He provides a suspiciously unemotional outline of his marriage and its breakdown, and appears to have avoided close ties with his son. He spends his vacations at his lakeside cottage with minimal human contacts, filling his days with the checking of meteorological observations, walking and rowing with his binoculars as constant companion, reading scientific books, solving chess problems and listening to classical music. A new math teacher, Gustafsson, disturbs the accustomed routine at the school by provocatively and systematically setting out to remind his colleagues of political and economic global injustices. He challenges the physics master by asking him if he goes in for concealed bourgeois indoctrination of his pupils, he puts up notices on the staff-room door about the decadence of the Western world, he speaks of the enslaved and starving masses and declares that on any given day at least ten thousand children will die of starvation. The physics master notes these activities in his diary and shows surprising tolerance toward Gustafsson. When another member of the staff says that he must be a Communist, the physics master retorts that their new colleague without any doubt is a painstaking and knowledgeable math teacher. One of Gustafsson's standing themes is the imminent inevitability of a world catastrophe— and here the book mirrors something of the apocalyptic mood of the year in which it was written, with the Vietnam War gathering momentum, violence erupting in Eastern Europe, and student riots shaking the West. He clearly foresees a nuclear holocaust, and enlivens his classes by demonstrating the mechanics of chain-reaction by means of ping-pong balls and mousetraps.

The physics master starts receiving mysterious phone calls; a voice, a different one each time, delivers a monologue.[6] The caller invariably describes an incident where he or she was engaged in a peaceful, normal pursuit which was suddenly shattered by a blinding white light, wind, and flames. The physics master immediately suspects Gustafsson of being behind the calls. The police advise him to unplug his phone at night, but when he follows this advice and is nevertheless wakened by its signals, his disturbed mental state is obvious to the reader, who also notes that as the days grow longer and the sharp spring light grows brighter, so his eyes become increasingly painful. He is clearly heading for a crisis, and his state of tense expectation is such that he feels disappointed when the phone rings and it turns out to be a normal call. In the midst of this he invites his son Harry to visit him during the summer holidays, and as the time approaches he actually looks forward to the encounter, and his colleagues say that he sounds "like a fellow who has just become a father" (223). But the night before the vacation starts, he receives a particularly gruesome phone call, a headache sets in, and he has the sensation of gravel in his watering eyes. The diary form precludes Evander from commenting on his protagonist's emotional experiences, but the swift change of mood undergone by the physics master indicates his inner conflict, which is soon to erupt. He fetches Harry at the station and they find difficulty in conversing naturally together. The father reacts with indignation when his son says, with evident indifference, that astronomy plays no part in his school syllabus. Nor is he interested in his father's diagrams of structural alterations to the cottage and declines the loan of binoculars. They row out on the lake, the father at the oars, overcome by a great feeling of fatigue. The boy explains that he has to leave the following day to stay with his mother, and when his father starts testing his knowledge of astronomy, he says that there are far more important problems in the world, adding that socialism is the only thing that can save the world from an impending disaster. Instead of answering his father's query about what sort of disaster, he lies in the stern of the boat, gazing down into the water. His father stops rowing, makes a vain attempt to regain his composure by training his binoculars upward toward some cloud formations, and then—when the boy persists in his silence—he stands up, disengages the binoculars, and hurls them at him, striking him on the back of the head. The boy's head and shoulders glide into the water, leaving him hanging over the side of the boat. His father's diary entry ends: "Harry's arms and head were lying almost entirely in the water. I stood gazing at him. I experienced a feeling of enormous fatigue" (225).

The Son. Before proceeding to an examination of the psychological and narrative questions associated with the above events, let us look at the boy Harry's engagingly slangy and humorous account of life at his folk high school. As we have already noted, folk high schools offer liberal courses not geared to examinations in a residential environment, designed for the spiritual and intellectual enrichment of students with no previous experience of higher education. Harry's enthusiasms and aggressions, his insecurity and growing-pains, are captured in teenage jargon both funny and authentic, reminiscent of the classic in the genre, *The Catcher in the Rye*, which was published in an excellent Swedish translation in 1968 and is acknowledged by Evander as a source of inspiration.[7] Harry is very small physically but makes up for this by a good head for mathematics and a terrier-like ability to hold his own. The canine association is apt, because Harry was the happy owner of a dachshund for eight childhood years, until it was run over to his inconsolable grief. His account of this event contrasts significantly with the detached one provided by his father, who is equally unable to identify with the shock felt by his pupils when a railway engine runs over a boxer puppy. Harry's lively account of life at school includes some hilarious episodes—for instance, the youngsters are hauled out on a dawn excursion by an unpopular biology mistress to hear the song of the bittern, very rare in that part of Sweden, when what they in fact hear, to her unsuspecting delight, is the noise produced by one of the boys blowing into an empty lemonade bottle. An elderly stand-in teacher is, by contrast, popular with the pupils: "On one occasion some second-year girls asked him if it wasn't difficult to give sex instruction in primary schools, but he said that it was far harder to jaw about Africa, where he'd never been" (211).

Harry looks at his fellow pupils and teachers with the clear, unsentimental eyes of youth, and he is loyal to both his divorced parents; his account demonstrates a sort of protective pity toward his mother, who remarries and in her son's eyes repeats her first matrimonial error: "Deep down, I believe she's married the wrong guy again. I feel sorry for ma in that way. She sure will always marry the wrong guy" (130). Harry himself is shy with girls, while the youth he shares a room with is so friendly with them that he lives in fear of finding himself a father. There are eager beavers and skivers, snobs and slobs, the gifted naturalist and the unprincipled lout who goes into town on Saturday night and on his way back seizes the hapless driver by the collar and spews down the back of his neck. The unvarnished picture of school life which emerges caused Göran Norström to inquire publicly whether Evander—in the centenary year of the folk high schools in Sweden—intended to imply that these institutions had had their day.[8] Evander replied as someone who had taught in two of these colleges and who was aware of the romantic nimbus attaching to them as gateways to learning for the eager and underprivileged.[9] Their present-day function, he maintained, was simply to provide preparatory courses for prospective nurses, policemen, and social workers. He added that the tone and language of Harry's descriptions was borrowed from letters and essays he had read during his time as a teacher.

Just as the physics master's diary ends with the scene in the rowing boat, so Harry's account of the same episode concludes the book. It will immediately be apparent that this is a highly problematic state of affairs, for how can he write an account of what appears to be his own death?

Narrative technique and irony. One way of solving the problem connected with the final act of violence would have been for the physics master alone to provide an account of how he threw his binoculars at Harry. Since, however, Evander has chosen the method of contrastive accounts by father and son, it is necessary for Harry, too, to describe their final encounter. His father, a lonely and repressed human being, has been driven to an act of lethal violence; Harry, on the other hand, is absorbed and happy at the end, for while his father harangues him about astronomy, he hangs over the stern of the boat, looking at the fishes swimming by, and then suddenly discovers that he can hear them sing. The beauty of this discovery lies in the fact that a friend has told him that fish sing when in shoals, because they like being together. While he is thus absorbed in the contemplation of togetherness, he is struck on the back of the head by his father's binoculars. His final words are: "for a short while I could actually hear them singing. I swear I could. And it sounded really swell, really goddam swell" (235).

The mystical nature of Harry's experience is clear, despite his colloquialisms. A number of Evander's novels end in analogous ways with an experience of timeless peace. Technically, the ending is flawed, since it breaks with the otherwise realistic conventions observed in the narrative, and it is arguable that Harry's enthusiasm for brotherhood, although attractive, has been insufficiently elaborated and thematized for it to support the poetic licence with which it is dignified. Evander himself may have had this in mind when he resisted the idea of a reprint, saying that he regards the book as a stage in his apprenticeship.[10]

Likeable as Harry may be, it is clear that his role is to throw his father into sharper relief. The *real* subject of the novel is the physics master's dangerous emotional repression. His diary is full of entries which, when correlated, prove that he consistently refuses to allow the pain of his marriage breakdown to surface. It is exactly the same phenomenon that Evander deals with, *mutatis mutandis*, in *Earth divine* seven years later. The inherent irony of the novel arises out of the fact that the physics master is unable or unwilling to draw the same inferences as the reader from his narrative. His consciousness cannot bridge the gulf between his declared good intentions and his actions, a case in point being his naive assertion that he has a keen eye for "the problems of youth" and is not unreceptive to humor "in suitable forms" (25), while he simultaneously quite fails to establish contact with his son. His ambition is to familiarize Harry with "our world picture . . . the universe, the multiplicity of riddles" (145), but it does not occur to him that the words "world picture" are more decisive when used metaphorically of how an individual sees himself in relation to other individuals, and that the manifold riddles of the human heart and emotions cry out for attention far more urgently than those of the astronomical universe.

A central focus for the novel's irony lies in the fact that a disaster does indeed strike the physics master, but not at all from the quarter he had anticipated. Structurally, the novel is built up round two axes of disaster, the one overt and explicit, the other covert and implicit. The former revolves round Gustafsson and his talk of world injustices and a threatened global disaster, the latter around the physics master's repressed emotions and his unsatisfactory relationships with his ex-wife and his son. He is fully aware of the Gustafsson axis, even to the extent of dreaming telephone calls about it, but he resists awareness of the latter. Every mysterious phone call the physics master receives describes an atomic war, i.e., a political and collective disaster. He should equally have been receiving signals from his own emotional system about a far more imminent personal disaster, but he is infinitely more resistant to the latter than the former. Gustafsson succeeds in goading him into some sort of awareness of global problems, but his own existential problem is too painful to be allowed to obtrude itself.

The interpretation offered here has as its corollary that the physics master was under such increasing emotional strain, for purely personal family reasons which have been discussed, that the political notion of a disaster propagated by Gustafsson supplied him with a threat—or promise—of release and relief through annihilation. It is as though his conscious mind would rather accept the escalating danger of military catastrophe than face the reality of an imminent nervous breakdown, and he focuses his anxieties on a pseudo-object instead of an authentic problem, witness the fantasy phone calls. In the final scene, his repressed bitterness and anger at his failure as husband and father overwhelm him and lead him to manslaughter.

The private versus public spheres. In reviewing Evander's book, the influential left-wing novelist P. O. Enquist suggests that Gustafsson by means of his agitation succeeds in making the physics master aware of the problems of the outside world and that the latter "does not know how to react to it. He slowly goes to pieces."[11] Enquist also suggests that Gustafsson makes him "start to think and question his own life."[12] But this is to maintain that Gustafsson's political message *in itself* is so potent that the physics master is changed by it and never recovers from it. Our contention in this study, by contrast, is that Gustafsson's activities provide the physics master with a substitute problem to project his anxieties onto. And we would argue that Gustafsson is shown as resorting to the generalities of politics in the same way as the physics master resorts to the abstractions of the astronomical universe. We are given a clue to the analogous nature of their preoccupations when the physics master writes of Gustafsson in his diary: "He is slandered in the staff room . . . . He himself slanders nobody, only people's views, or rather, their lack of them. I see him as a very 'pure' person" (72). Now by all the rules of discourse, if a fictional character (in this case a narrator) is presented ironically, if his judgment is defective (as the physics master's clearly is), then whatever he commends highly must in some sense be suspect. Evander has indicated in conversation that Gustafsson is drawn as typical of the period.[13] We need only cast our minds back to Göran Palm's books and articles and note that one of Gustafsson's dicta is that "an obsession with the private sphere is one of our most treacherous opiates" (128), whereas for Evander, awareness proceeds from the private to the general, or via the self to an increasing range of neighbors. Gustafsson's dismissal of the private sphere would destroy the very instrument of our perceptions.

Let us, finally, note Evander's words that the physics master's diary entries are "largely reproduced from an original—needless to say with the consent of the anonymous author."[14] We can safely assume that the diary was his own. The creative imagination does not produce a simple one-to-one correspondence between biographical data and fictional world, of course. As in the case of dreams, there has been "displacement" at work. But this is a book which presents an authentic existential dilemma in realistic terms, where *Close Relations* and *Dear Mr. Evander* were stylized and allegorical, and it indicates how interesting it will be to follow the development of the novels to come.

Chapter Three
Consolidation

The Upstarts—An Investigation

Uppkomlingarna—en personundersökning [The Upstarts—An Investigation] won for Evander in 1969 the prestigious annual literary prize offered by *Svenska Dagbladet.* It is not surprising that it was singled out, for it is an arresting and enigmatic work. The best way of approaching it is first to sketch a straightforward surface reading. A preface informs us that what follows is a report based on the posthumous papers and diaries of one Hadar Forsberg, ex-night watchman, subsequently turned writer, and on interviews with a number of people connected with him. To add to the air of authenticity, the author refers in a preface to the three occasions on which he met Forsberg. The tone is clinical throughout the book. No direct access is actually offered to the textual sources concerned, apart from occasional brief quotations in the body of the report. The narrator-investigator (who even within the framework of the fiction is named as Per Gunnar Evander) carefully controls and orders the information offered on the events leading up to the death of forty-year-old Forsberg, whose body is discovered in the cellar of the suburban Stockholm house where he lived alone after his wife had left him. Three years earlier, Forsberg had thrown up his job as night watchman when a book of his poems was accepted for publication. Shortly after that he met and married his wife, a prosperous schoolteacher with a marked respect for literary people and initially quite content to support a husband belonging to that category.

It is clear that Forsberg—goodlooking and attractive to women, although in other respects neither successful nor dynamic—is emotionally attached to his mother, and we are told that up to his marriage, he had had a large number of promiscuous and exclusively physical encounters with women. His wife was the first woman to whom he spoke of love, but their relationship deteriorates rapidly after their marriage. While he struggles unsuccessfully with his writing at home, he receives repeated visits from a ragged and hungry boy, soon to be joined by a number of other boys of varying ages and all sharing the same wretched condition. They claim, every one of them, to be Forsberg's illegitimate sons, and demand food and shelter in the warm basement boiler-room. On hearing who their respective mothers are, Forsberg concedes inwardly that they could be right about their paternity and makes only halfhearted attempts to get rid of them, although terrified that his wife will find out about them. In fact, she remains unaware of their existence, and as soon as she goes to stay with her mother as a form of separation from her husband, the boys invade the upper storeys of the house and carry off Forsberg to the cellar. Here they imprison him and subject him to systematic torture for a couple of months, until he dies of cold, neglect and the effects of their brutality.

The facts retailed above have been derived by the investigator from notes made by Forsberg before and during his imprisonment. The former makes it clear that Forsberg is the only person ever to have seen the boys and that his notes constitute our sole source of knowledge about them. The only corroborative evidence is that his putrescent body, when finally discovered in the deserted house, bore signs of "what could have been maltreatment"[189]. But neither Mrs. Forsberg, neighbors, the postman, nor the dustman could retrospectively call to mind anything to confirm or disprove the boys' existence. So the reader is left with the task of determining the ontological status of the various items of information detailed. Are they "true" or "false," "objective" or "subjective"? Was Forsberg mentally ill? The first step toward an answer must be to establish unambiguous facts about Forsberg, the second step to consider the boys, whose status is highly ambiguous.

Unambiguous facts:

1. **The stopwatch.** Forsberg is found dead with a stopwatch in his clenched fist. It is one of his most treasured possessions; he speaks of it as of an old friend and claims that it is "good for his nerves" (40). It is not hard to see that playing with a stopwatch is a symbolic way of controlling time and gaining illusory power. (Containing anxiety by means of ritual time-taking also features in the novel *A Love Story*, pp. 52–54.) When Forsberg's writing absorbs him, he

ceases to mention his watch, but when he gets stuck in his writing, he spends more and more time with the stopwatch, as he does on return from a holiday during which he has been grossly unfaithful to his fiancée. It functions as an indicator of tension. In this connection, we are told that Forsberg speaks of having cancer or a brain tumor whenever he is afflicted by a stomach or headache respectively, whereas a medical certificate from his watchman days pronounces him to be in good health, "apart from seemingly moderate hypochondria" (61).

2. **Relations with women.** The most affectionate words in Forsberg's diary concern his mother, and he weeps when his captors refuse to allow him to write to her, even secretly asking one of the boys to put an end to his life. She is quoted as saying of her son as a small child: "What I particularly remember is that Hadar was very docile and obedient" (11), and she quickly recovers from the shock of hearing about his death, deciding that it was all for the best in view of his disastrous marriage—she had steadfastly refused to meet her daughter-in-law after the wedding. In short, here is a son who fails to form a stable relationship with women other than his mother, to whom he is deeply—and, we may conjecture, unrequitedly—attached. Initially, his feelings for his wife seem promising, but instead of helping her when her father is dying of cancer, his own cancer phobia impels him to flee to a holiday resort where he takes up with an eighteen-year-old schoolgirl, who subsequently tells him that she is pregnant and on whom he induces an abortion. When his wife is told by the doctor that she cannot have children, she is deeply distressed, but he is incapable of comforting her and instead stresses how much he loves and longs for children.

3. **Forsberg's ambitions as a writer.** Throughout his working life as a watchman, Forsberg filled notebooks with his scribbling and dreamed of becoming a writer. But the investigator makes it clear that he was at a disadvantage, since critics were unfamiliar with his working-class contexts, he lacked literary contacts, his book had a romantic streak which was highly suspect in 1966, and he was unaware of the necessity for adapting to the literary climate: "He harbored the illusion that it would be enough to try to write as good a book as possible on the basis of his own experience. It was not

enough" (56). His poems, if reviewed at all, were damned with faint praise by critics whose minds were on other things. He next determines to write a documentary novel about a Swedish technical aid expert who sets out to save the Third World but is himself ultimately destroyed by the reality which surrounds him. Forsberg has been reading about "the state of the world" (83) (this phrase is to recur) in specialist studies of the global economic situation, and his ambition is to alert people to human misery and need. Before long he discovered how difficult it is to write about places unvisited and unfamiliar conditions and facts. A documentary account requires far more expertise than he has at his command. He decides to compose a book of poems instead, which will "say more than the novel ever could" (83), and a couple of months later he sends in a manuscript to his publishers, who politely but firmly reject it. So he decides to embark on a novel again, but his plans for it are only vaguely formulated. It is clear, however, that it is to be written in the first person, and a number of autobiographical episodes have been jotted down on scraps of paper.

It is at this point, when Forsberg has started work on his novel, that he is interrupted by the doorbell ringing—the first boy has arrived.

The ambiguous boys.   Forsberg's first reaction is to suspect a practical joke and he sends the boy away, but his concentration is broken, he begins to take long walks with stopwatch in hand and starts drinking, which causes arguments with his wife. As the weeks go by and an increasing number of boys occupy the cellar, he cannot sleep and is frightened that his wife should discover the intruders. Although he longs for her to move to her mother in the south of Sweden, he feels a sense of fear as soon as she has left and the threat posed by the boys suddenly looms large. He is not sure of their total number, but there are approximately ten of them, and they all have American names such as Lenny, Clifford, Steve, Clark, Tyrone, and so on. Despite their vengeful insolence, there is fear in their eyes, and perhaps the most notable fact about Forsberg's account of the cruelty to which they subject him is his total lack of resentment. Indeed, for some of them he feels positive tenderness. Even as they prepare to subject him to torture, he pats the cheek of one of them. In view of his lack of Christ-like attributes in other respects, his reaction is an unexpected one. It is clear that the reader has to exert himself in an attempt to interpret these events.

Let it be said straight away that the investigator, whose account we are reading, is unreliable. He claims to be putting the facts of the case squarely before us—but carefully inserted into his account are clues which—as we shall see—point in a direction to which he makes no reference. He fails to draw our attention to the most obvious solution to the problem of Forsberg's death; indeed, his presentation for all its apparent facticity is at this point in the narrative so insidiously persuasive that it seems likely that not a single first-time reader suspects that he is having the wool pulled over his eyes. What is so clever from the point of view of suspense and mystery, but so dissembling in a purportedly serious investigation, is that the narrator gives no hint that the chain of events he is unfolding is based on diary accounts of real events in Forsberg's life up to the fateful ringing of the doorbell, but on notes which constitute his novel from that moment onward.[1] There is absolutely no break in continuity and there is a great deal of skillful interlacing and cross-reference between these two sections. (Perhaps we may allow ourselves at this point to observe that the skill with which this literary deception is carried out is fully matched by that deployed by Evander eight years later when composing *The Snail* and *The Case of Lillemor Holm*, however much he may wish to deny it (cf. below, chapter 4). What supports the claim that the second half of *The Upstarts* constitutes Forsberg's novel, or rather, the investigator's retailing of his novel? It is a matter of drawing inferences. Let us rehearse them briefly. We have a man whose passionate desire it is to be a writer, but whose lack of education and experience has proved an unsurmountable obstacle to the writing of what both contemporary literary orthodoxy and political and economic realities favor, namely, a well-informed documentary novel. In addition, he has psychosexual problems. He has, for example, recently aborted an illegitimate child of his, soon after which his wife is found medically unable to bear children. This man is visited by a growing number of boys who claim—in one sense plausibly enough, in view of his promiscuity—to be his children. In view of the atrocities committed by them upon their father (and leaving out of account other cogent indications such as no traces of their occupation being found in the house after Forsberg's death, that the neighbors noticed nothing, that it would seem improbable that a dozen illegitimate sons born of different mothers would know about each other, and that the stopwatch was not taken from him), the reader is soon likely to decide that they have no concrete physical being and are figments of Forsberg's sick mind. P. O. Enquist, for instance, sees the book as "a study in insanity."[2] Other critics have suggested that Forsberg's ordeal at the hands of the boys could be an allegory of the deprived peoples of the Third World revenging themselves on Western man.[3] But both these readings leave out an absolutely central exegetical clue, namely, that Forsberg's primary aim in life is to succeed as a writer. And since it seems a reasonable assumption that the interpretation which exploits a novel's potentialities the most is the one to be favored, it is our contention that Forsberg, wishing to write about the problems of the Third World, but being precluded from doing so objectively, does so in the only way he can—by relating *imaginatively* to his subject and by utilizing the autobiographical material at his disposal.

If we accept this premise, we recollect that Forsberg had children on his mind in a guilt-ridden way. Hungry, illegitimate sons—so dirty as to appear almost "dark-skinned" (142)—demanding food and restitution, are a good metaphor for starving and resentful fellow humans in the developing countries. Their American names provide another link with the Third World, by an association with the random offspring of American troops in Korea and Vietnam (a sort of parallel to Forsberg's progeny).[4] It is certainly no coincidence that the cellar both represents a place of punishment and—in Freudian terms—the subconscious. It is from his subconscious, from the storehouse of memory, that Forsberg derives the material for his novel. Although not widely read, he had, for instance, derived much pleasure from Vergil's *Aeneid*, particularly its description of Hades. He had, indeed, called his only published book *Confessions from the Underworld*. Assuming, therefore, that the boys have sprung from guilt feelings over aborted fetuses nightmarishly grown into avengers, then the fear in their eyes reflects their experience of being ousted from the warm safety of the womb, and in terms of Rhadamanthine punishment befitting the crime,[5] it is meet that Forsberg the aborter and philanderer should be banished from his warm home to the cold cellar and be subjected to beatings by steel cables (the instrument he used for abortion being a flexible metal rod and the skill with which he performed the operation on the schoolgirl indicating considerable practice in the art). Vergil tells us that in Hades "souls are ceaselessly schooled by retribution, and pay in punishment for their old offences," some hapless sinners being "hung, stretched and helpless," while the wickedness of others is "burnt out of them by fire."[6] Forsberg, for his part, is hung from a carpet-beating rack by his knees, and burned by a blow-lamp.

It is at this point that one of the boys tells him that they are proud to have a father "whose condition mirrors the state of the world" (174), adding that very few people in their country have such a parent. If we allow that Forsberg in writing his novel wants to communicate an insight into global injustice and suffering, but that he is unable to do so by means of a wide grasp of facts and figures—in the manner of, say, Göran Palm—then using his own guilt and penitential suffering as a metaphor is the next best thing. And it is certainly, as the boys suggest, a rare phenomenon. In fact, by the end Forsberg not only metaphorically but also literally mirrors the starving masses by dying. The few bank notes left by his wife on the kitchen table cannot go far. All that is found in the frigidaire when his decomposing body is discovered in the cellar is half a carton of sour milk. Once his novel gets under way (once, that is, the boys have imprisoned him in the cellar), he "lives" his story so vividly that he merges with his fiction. The investigator says that all traces of his customary hypochondria vanish. Forsberg now ascribes aches and pains—which we must suppose are in reality pains of hunger and weakness—not to tumors and cancer but to beatings and burnings, in other words, his present suffering is meaningful since it has a creative function and furthers his literary work, which leads him to feel no resentment toward those who inflict it on him but rather a form of gratitude.

The parallel with *The Myth of Wu Tao-Tzu*. A vivid sensory impression experienced by Forsberg remains to be explained. It is a white landscape which is so brilliant that "it bursts into flame and envelops him with its heat and its beauty and does not leave him until it chooses to depart" (186). This image is the final one noted by the dying man, who is now so weak that he can hardly hold a pencil. He no longer speaks of his novel, nor of the cold, nor of his "bad memories" (187). He has been absorbed into the white landscape in a mystical union.

Intellectual and literary circles in Sweden were much taken, in 1967, with a book by Sven Lindqvist entitled *Myten om Wu Tao-tzu* [The Myth of Wu Tao-Tzu]. Written discursively in the first person, it traces the author's relationship to the work and philosophy of Herman Hesse, and the short story in which Hesse paints a small landscape on his cell wall, and then—like the Chinese artist Wu Tao-Tzu—steps into it and disappears from view.[7] This image of the artist withdrawing into his art, after years of training and high-minded spiritual exertion, was Lindqvist's ideal until his awakening, in the stormy 1960s, to the scale of human suffering in the underprivileged areas of the globe. After visits to China and India, he wrote *The Myth of Wu Tao-Tzu* which ends with the writer sitting cross-legged and covered with a layer of gold, an eternally smiling and passive Buddha. Lindqvist's indictment of art for art's sake—or indeed for any principle's sake other than that of actively shouldering political responsibility—is quite explicit, and was shown to be unequivocal when he followed it up in 1969 by the first of two painstaking, firsthand factual reports on oppression and poverty in South America.[8] What no one seems to have noticed is that Evander's subtle and *un*explicit novel is another version of the artist disappearing into his own picture: first, when Evander— by means of a brilliant narrative trick halfway through *The Upstarts*—lets his main character Forsberg be absorbed into the novel he himself is writing, and second, when Forsberg, as he lies dying, is drawn into a hallucinatory white landscape. Forsberg chooses to identify *with* poverty and hunger rather than identifying *them* by means of socio-economic analysis.

Looked at in this light, *The Upstarts* can be seen as a response to Lindqvist's challenge. It is tempting to see it as combining the twin "suspect" properties aesthetic elaboration and individual emotional involvement on the one hand, with the "respectable" documentary form on the other. Furthermore, it seems to demonstrate the belief that an individual's subjective reactions, suffering, and redemption *are* important, despite the literary climate of the day.

Concealing and revealing. Evander's public utterances about his work tend to act as both smoke screen and smoke signals. The persistent enquirer can discern both effects. Consider, for example, his observation that his novel *The Last Day of Valle Hedman's Life* was "planned as the third and last part of the trilogy which began with *The Upstarts*. My primary aim with these three books . . . was to describe everyday conditions of manual labor and somehow demonstrate the way in which this work may have affected its practitioner."[9] Noting that the only manual labor described in *The Upstarts* is the brief account of Forsberg's employment as a night watchman, whereas the remaining two books of the trilogy do in a most obvious way deal with bodily labor, we may shrug the remark off as a mystification. But supposing this in fact is a signal saying that the book describes the conditions of *the author's* working life, which indeed affected its practitioner to the point of undermining his very survival. Seeing Forsberg's experience as an extreme example of the bodily as well as mental suffering associated with creative writing ties in with Evander's declaration that he himself when writing is an "extremely unhappy person" and that sitting at his typewriter is a form of "manual labor which gives me backache."[10] This would certainly appear to explain why he has not devoted himself entirely to writing, although his part-time output matches that of many a full-time author. The physical and psychological strain of creative literary work, with its attendant loneliness, clearly needs to alternate with spells of extrovert action. These reflections have a bearing on his next novel, which seems, in a most interesting way, both to be about a collective social activity (brickmaking) and—again—about the situation of the artist.

Foreman Lundin of the Brickworks and the Wide World

During his year of casual labor in 1956 after completing national service, Evander met the owner of a local brickworks, who offered him a short-term job. In 1968, Evander, having completed a course for television producers, was invited to contribute a film presenting a

Swedish industrial enterprise for a series entitled *The Innovators*. His erstwhile employers Sandvikens Ironworks, whom he first approached, declined to cooperate, but the brickworks owner was willing, and Evander took a camera crew with him and made a film about this small business, which was on the point of closing down. Not only that, in 1970 he published the novel *Tegelmästare Lundin och stora världen* [Foreman Lundin of the Brickworks and the Wide World], and in 1976 he wrote a play, *The Goldfish*, with the same background.

The novel's motto encapsulates the proposition that "a picture simply cannot function without help [from words]" (133). As befits such a view, the slim volume of one hundred and sixty pages consists solely of words describing sixty-one numbered—and unseen—photographs, taken in and around the brickworks. The text not only conjures up the visual image but also tells us how each picture came to be taken, and frequently includes a revelation that its face value is diametrically opposed to the reality of what is portrayed. Evander is too sensitive a writer to let all the photographs lie, but the majority of them travesty the underlying reality. Two laughing girls who look like the incarnation of happy youth are in fact struggling respectively with leukemia and an unwanted pregnancy; two acknowledged enemies are seen with their arms round each other's shoulders (an ironic pose? not even the narrator claims to know the truth); a smiling worker seated on a fork-truck is being subjected to levels of dust and noise which the photograph can give no indication of. We are constantly reminded of how little we know about the lives of our fellow humans—and how much more we *could* know if we exerted ourselves.

The brickworks is a small inherited family enterprise, which after a minor boom in the early 1960s is now being forced out of business by cheaper bricks from Denmark and Poland and increasing use of concrete in the building trade. Without weighing down his narrative, Evander provides facts and figures. There are around twenty workers employed in the manufacture of the bricks, and we see the man excavating and loading clay from a nearby pit and the men who unload it, mix it, feed it into machines, cut the stream of wet clay into segments, load the wet bricks and transport them to a shed for drying, move them on to ovens for baking, and, finally, load them onto trucks for dispatch. The narrator describes his own employment there as a twenty-year old, the heavy and monotonous work involved in loading and driving a fork-truck with half a ton of wet bricks, a process repeated one hundred and twenty times a day. The strain on arms and back was punishing, but the first lesson one learned was not to complain. Most of the workers had been there for years and accepted the dust and noise and physical strain, with attendant ill effects, as facts of life. All of them are marked in one way or another by their daily toil, by rheumatism and ruined backs, but their patience and loyalty is extraordinary. Not even the one Communist party member among them is politically active. Evander succeeds in bringing these people and their families to life by means of small stories and anecdotes, and he does so with contagious affection. As a solitary example, let us take the aging Folke Strid, who gets overrefreshed on a visit to the local town, and makes an affectionate advance to the woman sitting next to him on a bench, finding her unexpectedly beautiful in the light of the setting sun. She, for her part, roundly rebukes him and the exchange is overheard by a zealous young policeman who

is not satisfied until the law-abiding and unsuspecting Strid has accompanied him to the police station.

Here Strid's name and occupation are noted and he naturally explains that the object of his sudden passion in fact is his lawful wedded wife of forty years' standing. This assurance, which is instantly verifiable at the scene of the crime, does not prevent Strid from later on being found guilty of disorderly conduct and fined fifty crowns.

It was typical of Strid that he still many years later looked very seriously upon this miscarriage of justice at the bus terminal square in Gävle. (96)

The dubious validity of the visual image. The majority of the photographs have been taken by one Axel Schröder, ex-employee of the works and enthusiastic amateur photographer, who has lived for some years after throwing up his laboring job in happy commitment to his new pursuit and in the conviction of his own artistic talent, scraping a meager living by occasionally selling pictures and otherwise relying on the generosity of the narrator's parents, who have given him a home. Foreman Lundin of the works is also a devotee of the photographic image, but with the crucial difference that he—a born raconteur—makes the pictures in his huge collection mean anything he wants them to by dint of his verbal skill—and significantly, he never shows any of his pictures unless he simultaneously has the opportunity of exercising his "almost spellbinding gift as a narrator" (76), for, as he frequently remarks, an undirected image is meaningless. On one of the photographs from the brickworks we see him

> explaining and gesticulating. . . . He really moves with the confidence and solidity of a man of the world. He knows how to behave to his boss, customers, and employees. He is a man who has seen the world and knows what bricks are called in most of the major languages.
>
> But fifteen yards away behind the walls of the machine shop there are folks who know that he has never seen the sea except in photographs. (104-5)

The truth is, quite simply, that Lundin suffers from an anxiety neurosis which makes him acutely dependent on his wife and prevents him from going further afield from the works than at the most three or four miles. Schröder, who has for years believed implicitly in Lundin's stories of wars, journeys, and far-away places, falls prey to a deep depression when he learns that there is not a shred of truth in them—and burns his own collection of photographs (with the exception of the limited number rescued by the narrator). He never recovers his spirits, and not long afterward he dies in hospital, with the narrator holding his hand.

The role of the artist.   Quite clearly, this novel has two strands: the lives of the workers on the one hand, and the drama set up by the conflicting claims of the visual image and the spoken (or written) word on the other. The presentation of the brickworkers has been compared, with some justification, to Edgar Lee Masters' *Spoon River Anthology,* in the sense that both works provide a portrait gallery of a small community.[11] But we need to ask ourselves why foreman Lundin gives his name to the book and what the real nature of his relationship to Schröder is. Both men suffer from anxiety neuroses, but their respective responses differ: Schröder is a hypochondriac, while Lundin manages to "bury" his anxiety, so that outwardly all that shows is its symptom, namely, his mythomania. Lundin's workmates—with the notable exception of Schröder—realize that his compelling stories are a form of compensation for his basic insecurity. But this does not prevent them from respecting him. It seems fair to class both the hypochondriac and the mythomaniac as artists within the sign language of the book. Schröder came to photography late in life, and embraced it with naive faith, convinced that he had a calling and a gift. His artistic shortcomings are described with the same sympathy that Evander accorded to the work of Hadar Forsberg, another dedicated but unsuccessful member of the species artist. It is probably also significant that Evander bestows a number of his own characteristics on Schröder: a late starter, no head for heights, not lacking "an eye for human beings" (39) (phrase originated by the writer C.J.L. Almqvist and adopted by Evander),[12] and not knowing what is meant by "visual flair" (142) (a fashionable cliché which Evander has publicly and repeatedly expressed his dislike of).[13]

We might guess that Schröder and Lundin are manifestations of a conflict within Evander himself about how to resolve his role as artist and ask ourselves if the media man Evander was already disillusioned after only two years of working for television? It seems more likely that he uses photographs/images as a metaphor for art in a broad sense, and that his concern is with the existential problem of the artist's attitude to his art.

The crucial difference between Schröder and Lundin is that Schröder has allowed himself to be ruled by his belief in the absolute value of the image (art) and has devoted himself entirely (and uncomprehendingly) to it, until his fatal misunderstanding of its whole nature is made clear to him—a discovery he is unable to bear. Both Schröder and Forsberg (of *The Upstarts*), threw up their regular jobs as soon as a minor artistic success gave them the unrealistic idea of living only as artists—and both go under. As does Leonardsson, a photographer in Evander's first television film, who lives for twenty years on the myth that he is an artist until one day he discovers that "all pictures basically represent the same thing and that one word says more than a thousand pictures."[14] Foreman Lundin, on the other hand, has never harbored any illusions about the magic status of the image (art), but uses it for his own purposes of flights of narrative fiction in intervals between his periods of highly efficient bread-and-butter activity. My suggestion is that he represents the manner in which Evander has come to terms with his role as artist: rejecting romantic, full-time dedication and instead alternating active, participatory pursuits with lonely spells of writing.

It needs to be said that Evander himself has only indirectly contributed to this exegesis of his novel, oddly enough by protesting too much:

My aim in *Foreman Lundin* was to describe a works about to be closed down. Describe the hell the brickworkers endured and largely still endure. The book is an ordinary story, even although I juggled a bit with the form. Typically, critics in the big dailies concentrated on the book's form and *some relatively unimportant discussions on how to interpret images.* In provincial papers, on the other hand, particularly in Uppland, Skåne, and Gästrikland, where there are many brickworks, it was regarded as *a political novel.*[15] (Italics added here).

Foreman Lundin's value as a "political" novel is naturally not diminished by the fact that it is also a projection of its author's continued grappling with the problems associated with the role of an artist. But we would do well to remember that it was still almost a requirement to write in the documentary or sociological vein in the Sweden of 1970. Perhaps this explains why Evander, in the remarks quoted above, stresses that his book provides a picture of working life, and why he was so touchy when responding to a review of his book by the critic Bengt Holmqvist, who spoke of *Foreman Lundin* (and *The Upstarts*) as a "quasi-documentary novel on a high intellectual and artistic level."[16] Evander protested at the prefix *quasi* and complained of the reviewer that he

almost provocatively takes it for granted that the novel about foreman Lundin, in common with my novel from last year about the upstarts round Hadar Forsberg, is "quasi-documentary." He does it automatically and without any attempt at justification. . . .

Holmqvist presupposes, in other words, that the narrator is not in all respects identical with the author. The same assertion was made in certain quarters about my preceding book [*The Upstarts*], particularly with regard to the actual introduction.

But why could I not have been employed at a brickworks outside Gävle when I was twenty, why could I not have run four hundred meters in 51.2 as a junior, why could not all these workers have been at this brickworks at this particular point in time?[17]

Why not indeed? But what about the personal data which do *not* fit? The working-class parents and the brother with whom the narrator has been provided? What about Schröder and Lundin? What about the twenty-two fictive (as it turns out) workers' names to whom the book is dedicated?

Evander goes on to say that the interesting thing is not whether a book of his is wholly or only partially documentary, but whether the documentary *form* functions well. There can only be one answer to that. It functions perfectly in this book, as in his next (in which he studiously avoids introducing a personal narrator).

The Last Day of Valle Hedman's Life

A brief prefatory note to *Sista dagen i Valle Hedmans Liv* [The Last Day of Valle Hedman's Life] explains that Valle Hedman, sheet-metal workshop owner, fell to his death from a roof in November 1970. A meticulous investigation into the circumstances surrounding the accident was commissioned by the police and the Council for Industrial Safety, and hinged on information supplied by two of Hedman's employees present at the time of the accident. Their testimony forms the basis of the reconstruction of events which constitutes the novel. This all sounds very factual and documentary. But it is, of course, a novel—and Evander offers the following information on the book's back cover:

On one level this novel is simply about how a sheet-metal worker has a fatal accident in the course of his in many ways exacting craft. The situation is somewhat complicated by the fact that he runs his own business, and it has been my aim not only to describe the daily round of manual labor but also the death-throes of a small firm in the Sweden of today. It is possible . . . that something else is happening on another level, perhaps even on several other levels. But it is of course up to the reader to decide that.

The power of this little book, just one hundred and forty pages long, lies in the interaction of the various levels mentioned by Evander, whereby technical data on the sheet-metal trade merge with the human interest elicited by the characters. The only thing we know for certain is that Valle Hedman is going to die; everything else about the people involved is fresh and frequently mystifying—and it is this element of mystery or uncertainty which constitutes the other level or levels. Or to put it another way, the logic of Evander's narrative about Valle Hedman is never in doubt—i.e., the indefensible strain of piecework in a hazardous occupation—the uncertainty arises on the level of personalities and relationships.

Hedman's wife exemplifies the uncertain element. The chief witness, one Persson, mentions two domestic altercations between the Hedmans, and he also mentions having inadvertently seen Mrs. Hedman naked in the bathroom, through the open door, when he returned to the house unexpectedly to fetch a pair of gloves at her husband's request. The text is so ambiguously open that it can be construed in a variety of ways. Hedman could have sent Persson back with the express aim in mind of letting him have an encounter with his wife; it is certainly very strange that he never uses the gloves, once they are handed to him. The lady may or may not have heard Persson arrive. The incident could also simply be indicative of his own poorly repressed interest in her. We are told that the other witness was in fact commonly thought to have had an affair with Mrs. Hedman some time before, since when their relations have been icily formal. It also appears from the narrative that Hedman and his wife have separate bedrooms. Here is food for speculation—as there is at the close of the book, when Persson has the heavy task of returning to the Hedman's house in order to tell Mrs. Hedman that her husband has just been killed. He pauses in the garden and once again, himself unseen, he observes her, this time through the kitchen window, as she prepares for their afternoon break. He does not know what to say to her, but plucks up courage and rings the doorbell. "Just a few seconds later Hedman's wife opens the front door and at the very same moment, according to Persson, he feels the smell of freshly-brewed coffee well over him" (145). And here the book closes. We are left with the welcoming smell and our unanswered queries about what happened next.

The art—and artifice—with which the story is told links up with Evander's remark that the more significance you attach to your message, the more vital the question of form becomes.[18] In his view, contemporary Swedish political theater was making the mistake of tiring audiences by nonchalant disregard of their legitimate need for entertainment as well as instruction.

Countdown to death. The countdown to Hedman's death generates increasing narrative tension as zero hour approaches. We know he is going to die, but we do not know how. Evander has adopted the device of the foregone death from a short story, "To Kill a Child," by Stig Dagerman. In it, a small child, dispatched on an errand by its mother, and a young couple motoring down to the seaside, are shown inexorably moving toward the fatal moment of impact. In both works, the effect builds on the protagonists' total unawareness of what is to come.

Harsh realities. By the end of the book, the reader has experienced something of what it is like to be under continual stress—in a job which you basically enjoy—except for contingent pressures, what it is like not to have time to look after your health or to rest your bad leg, to be continually faced with the threat of bankruptcy and the overwhelming competition of big firms. The witness Persson has seen his employer spewing violently but had his suggestion that he ought to see a doctor rudely rejected: "That's easy for you to say! Tell it to an employee. When you're running your own show you can't afford to keep running to the bloody doctor!" (39) Hedman is clearly worried by outstanding bills and has worked all through the weekend before the fatal Monday of the accident. He starts relaying the tin roof of a local school without—for reasons of economy—putting up a safety barrier at the base of the roof or taking any of the other prescribed precautions.

In a sense, Hedman is "asking for it." In another and more important sense, he is the victim of an industrial and social development which places an intolerable burden of paperwork, taxes, and insurance on the self-employed entrepreneur, who by training and inclination is a craftsman with neither taste nor time for the bookkeeping and bureaucracy he is forced to submit to. The book is prefaced by an authentic quotation from a leaflet issued by the Central Employment Board: "Sheet-metal work in the building trade is a congenial occupation. The work is independent and varied. With good basic training and practical experience of various types of job you can earn good money as a sheet-metal worker, since 80 percent of the work is piecework. What is more, if you are hardworking and enterprising, you can train as a foreman, surveyor, etc.,—or maybe even start a business of your own" (7).

The entire novel demonstrates the falsity and cynicism of this recruitment propaganda. Hedman and his employees all suffer from occupational stress and ailments. In addition to having bad backs and stomachs, the employees feel hounded by piece rates, while the small employer is haunted by fear of financial ruin. These insights are conveyed, not by overt social or political criticism, but by cumulative inference derived from concrete evidence, of whose significance the witnesses themselves seem scarcely aware. On the contrary, they accept their difficulties as facts of life, and their accounts of the tragedy are ingenuously directed toward charting only the immediate and outward chain of events preceding the actual fall.

We see three men working on a roof made slippery by rain and oil on a dark, drizzly November day, exchanging a few words, arguing about their favorite ice-hockey teams. We learn something about the personal circumstances of each of them. And all the while, we are aware that at 2:45 P.M., just a quarter of an hour before Hedman and Persson are due to drive back home for their coffee break, Hedman is going to have a fatal accident. When it comes, it takes the reader almost as much by surprise as the two employees. There is a sudden thump on the tin roof and Hedman lies spread-eagled on the upper level of the mansard roof. There is nothing for him to grasp, he starts sliding down the roof, gradually gathering momentum, and his stunned employees watch helplessly as he disappears over the edge. A few seconds later a thud indicates that he has landed on the cemented yard thirty-six feet below. The enormity of the shock experienced by both witnesses is indicated by the fact that neither of them can immediately bring himself to hurry down to help Hedman. We assume that they both know he is dead, and that the fear they have to repress daily, in order to go on working, has been released—with paralyzing effect.

Evander acquired his knowledge of sheet-metal work during his spell as a teacher at Gästrikland's folk high school. A colleague was married to a sheet-metal workshop owner and roof-layer, and Evander—having a light teaching load—started helping in the workshop and making himself useful in a variety of ways, although his poor head for heights prevented him from actually working on roofs.

The hideous anecdote. Persson recalls an anecdote told him by Hedman. Half a century ago his baby brother had died of tuberculosis, and had been laid out in the woodshed prior to the funeral. A party of drunken company directors appear on the scene, and after some clumsy condolences they ask Hedman's mother if they can buy the baby as eel-bait, for which they would pay well, since nothing tempts eels more than tender human flesh. The poor woman's natural respect for her social superiors, as well as her poverty, lead her to reflect a few minutes before humbly declining the offer. Her husband sits silent and motionless throughout. The witness Persson adds that he got the impression that Hedman was talking about himself in some way.

It is not difficult to interpret Hedman's story. Admittedly, drunken directors are unlikely, in our day, to put such crude propositions to their fellow humans, but in the interests of structural reorganization and profit-maximizing, a highly industrialized society may yet exact a mortal toll from its powerless victims. The symbolic truth of this parable, which is said to come from an old wives' tale from Åshammar in central Gästrikland, evidently so etched itself into Evander's consciousness as a supreme example of the humiliation of the poor by the powerful that he used it again in his television film *Cheating* (1978).

Despite excellent reviews, *Foreman Lundin* sold only some 1,100 copies in its first year. In an attempt to reach a wider readership, Evander published *The Last Day of Valle Hedman's Life* in paperback through the Writers' Publishing Co-operative (Författarförlaget). Sales topped 4,000, which may not be many compared to the figures reached by his best-selling novels from 1973 onward, but was nevertheless an improvement. The book aroused widespread interest, and a Gothenburg paper arranged a competition for the best amateur reviews of it, attracting three hundred and thirty entries.[19] Five months later, a new book by Evander appeared in which the impersonal facticity of *Valle Hedman* was replaced by subjectivity. The juxtaposition is arresting and tells us a lot, both about Evander's desire to help to improve the lot of manual workers on the one hand, and his powerful urge for self-exploration on the other.

A Love Story

En kärleksroman [A Love Story] is the account of the different strategies in life adopted by two brothers. The first-person narrator is called Per Gunnar Evander, a producer for Swedish Television. His younger brother Henning is identical with the narrator's brother in *Foreman Lundin*. Hindsight and analysis lead to the conclusion that the brothers represent projections of the author's personality—which has been confirmed by him in a radio interview[20]—but young Henning is provided with so convincing a personality and social framework that on an initial reading he comes over as a totally independent character in the fictive world of the novel. This fact was pleasantly confirmed by a number of reviewers, who quite straightforwardly accepted the two brothers as separate individuals[21] (but see sectional postscript below, for an opposite view). Any reader familiar with Evander's appearance will recognize much of the description of Henning as according closely with it.

Henning has been in trouble with the law because of an act of senseless violence against an old couple during his teens, and he is unmistakably at a disadvantage compared to his older brother. He now works as a filling-station attendant. Yet in other ways he has had a fuller life than Per Gunnar; he was engaged for over a year and has a daughter with his ex-fiancée, and during the limited span of the novel he is shown warmth and kindness by two girls with whom he successively lives for short periods. He also falls passionately in love with a young married woman, Anna, who finally fails to keep her promise to leave her husband.

His brother Per Gunnar's life, on the other hand, is bounded by his office at the Swedish Broadcasting Corporation and his writing desk at home; we hear of no girl friends and no relaxations. From time to time Per Gunnar allows Henning to stay with him in his flat and dispenses big-brotherly advice. He is patently in command of his own life, unlike his younger brother. Notwithstanding this fact, Henning has the temerity to tell him that his novels lack sensuality and that he himself is going to write a novel with far more warmth and emotional commitment than his older brother has ever succeeded in doing. This ambition is never realized, however, so utterly absorbed is he in the turmoil of his love for Anna. As he puts it, "you can't write a love story . . . when you're in the middle of it yourself," and then, looking at his brother, "I wonder if you understand what it really feels like" (166). Toward the end of the book he appears outwardly to have recovered from the pain of being rejected by her, but after a cheerful evening *à trois* with another girl friend and the narrator, he drives out to a snow-bound cottage and swallows a bottleful of sleeping tablets, leaving beside him a sheet of paper with the words: "I want to be with Anna" (210).

Ostensibly about the relationship between two brothers and implicitly about aspects of the author's personality, this novel is ultimately about the creative artist's existential dilemma: how to reconcile private life and art. Henning's inability to handle the situation when Anna rejects him ultimately proves fatal to him. Kind as the young women are with whom he lives, his death is the outcome of his relationship with one of them. In that sense Per Gunnar's policy of self-preservation by keeping women at arms' length is justified, we must suppose. As he says rather patronizingly in response to his younger brother's agonized query about Anna: "But what would you have done?"—"I would never have got myself involved in anything like this" (173).

The crux of the matter is whether Henning's claim to be able to write a far richer book than Per Gunnar is taken seriously. Evander's book three novels on from this one—*Mondays with Fanny* (1974)—constitutes a breakthrough in terms of a presentation of reciprocal love and warmth between a man and a woman. At this time it was still a problem. When asked in a radio interview about Henning's claim that Per Gunnar was unable to write about women in love, Evander replied that the charge had often been leveled at him that his novels lacked warm-blooded women and that he altogether dealt summarily with women—as opposed to men. "I think that's quite wrong, because it is most frequently women I am writing about, even if the books are about men, so to speak,"[22] he continued, and went on to speak of the works environment in which he grew up, where people "more or less took a pride in not showing their feelings, where a mark of affection was often . . . not even a thump on the shoulder but maybe a jeer or a swear-word . . . you never dared to show or say anything that expressed tenderness in conventional terms."[23]

The bird and the situation of the artist. *A Love Story* is provided with a leitmotiv immediately visible on the book's front cover in the shape of a small grey caged bird against a red background. The original painting hangs on a wall in Evander's home. He had seen and admired it at an exhibition, and in the summer of 1970 the artist, Louis Lindholm, made him a present of it. The painting seems to have played a central role in inspiring and determining the symbolism of the novel. Evander let his imagination play on the painting and all that the novel tells us of the picture's inception and execution is derived from his fantasies (and not from the artist's actual experiences, whatever these may have been). The image of a bird as a symbol of longing is familiar—one might say archetypical—in Swedish literature, and derives from the return of migratory birds as harbingers of spring to the frozen North, as well as a reminder of happier climes when autumn darkness closes in.[24] This little grey bird represents longing incarnate. Initially, the canvas was simply painted with an orange background and the artist toyed with the idea of painting a realistic portrait, so the novel tells us, but abandoned it in favor of capturing a situation, "possibly that of a human being, not necessarily his own, but maybe that too" (56). At rhythmically regular intervals the narrative reverts to Lindholm and his progress. He changes the background color, the whole time following his instinct, avoiding deliberate control of his motif. We witness a creative process without the artist's conscious intervention, and just as disturbed patients reveal their problems when provided with paper and watercolors, so we must assume that Lindholm reveals the existential situation of the artist— for this is really what the book is about.

He is responsive to nature, he sits in his garden inhaling summer scents and listening intently to the bird song, and then gradually as winter comes, he starts to paint a small grey bird on his canvas. Later on he feels disturbed lest the bird should fly off into the dark red space surrounding it, and in order to free himself from this continuous distraction he paints a small silver-grey cage around it. When he starts painting, it is a glorious Indian summer, and he keeps telling his wife that he longs to get out of his studio: "But Lindholm *knows that he is lying* . . . because all the truth he can muster has to be devoted solely and entirely to his painting" (29; my italics). He is free to go wherever he wants to; but he places an invisible cage around himself in order to be able to function as an artist. The symbolism is elaborated when Per Gunnar, after Henning's death, walks across a sun-lit frozen lake and is assailed by "an immensely powerful longing to walk alone in the sunshine across a lake on a winter's day . . . as I was doing just then" (210). Or to spell it out, Lindholm was deceiving himself when he said he wished to be elsewhere than in his studio. And Per Gunnar wishes to be precisely where he is, *alone* on a white expanse of snow— a striking image of a writer's self-imposed isolation.

The theme of longing coexisting with its own fulfillment is introduced on a very mundane level early in the book. A girl student at a folk high school declares that she longs to eat boiled cod. Since this is precisely what she is doing at the time, she occasions her listeners some mirth, which she counters fiercely by declaring that it is indeed possible to long for something already in one's possession. The notion is taken up again when Henning says that he longs for Anna even when she is there with him (144). Evander's handling of the theme evidently struck a chord with his Swedish readers, witness the following quotation from Gun-Britt Sundström's novel *Maken* [My other half]. The narrator, on board a yacht, has returned to base, a peaceful bay:

Here, I thought, is where one ought to cast anchor for the night on a silent summer's night. Upon which I naturally thought of Per Gunnar Evander, as any educated person would in similar circumstances (as though he had patented the discovery that you can long to do precisely what you are doing; the experience is presumably familiar to most people in this neurotic age, it's only that he happens to have become famous for having described it that makes you think of him if you're a well-read person).[25]

There are other variations on the theme of longing: an old aunt has to marshal her memories into the good and the bad ones, a process bound up with retrospective longing, we are told; a schoolgirl drowns herself because of unhappy love; Per Gunnar's father figures in a couple of anecdotes, which show him, all rigged out with bird chart and binoculars, to be afflicted with a strong sense of disappointed longing.

The most striking bird image is associated with the journalist Göran Norström, Evander's friend, who figures in the novel. This fictive Norström can charm the birds out of the trees, right up to his open french windows, when he plays a melody of his own on the piano. His whole garden becomes crowded on these occasions with birds of all kinds, who perch on the verandah rail to get as close as possible to the music. In the early hours of one morning Per Gunnar, who together with his brother is staying as a guest in the house, wakes up to find his host playing the spell-binding melody "and hissing like a snake" (59), while Henning, without a stitch of clothing on him, is dancing slowly behind the pianist, "like a naked god" (59), with a tall, lighted candle in one hand. The narrative offers no interpretation of the scene. A Satanic seduction, suggested by the reptilian reference in conjunction with the alluring tune? Seeing the pianist Norström as a latter-day Orpheus makes better sense in conjunction with Henning's Dionysian ecstasy and the phallic associations of the candle. Certainly we are being shown two men—each in their own way representing an artist— in touch with the deep wellspring of emotion. The other type of artist—the Apollonian variety—is represented by the detached, serene attitudes of Lindholm and Per Gunnar.

Everything about this carefully planned and executed novel suggests that what distinguishes the two brothers is the emotional spontaneity of the one and the cerebral control of the other. Henning's powers of extrasensory perception illustrate this. He is able to guess or "sense" the suit and value of concealed playing cards and the contents of purses with a high degree of accuracy, and this ability gives him great satisfaction. Per Gunnar has no such paranormal ability.[26] The theme of clairvoyance recurs as an important element in the novels *The Snail* and *The Case of Lillemor Holm*. Suffice it to say here that in this novel the ability seems characteristic of Henning as a human being in touch with those inner resources, from which a higher degree of control and awareness might cut him off.

Longing and politics. When a big daily paper ran a series of articles on human characteristics and states of being in the summer of 1971, Evander chose to write about the state of longing, since he had recently come to the realization that the novel—*A Love Story*—which he was just finishing, "to a large and perhaps crucial extent actually deals with what we normally understand by the term [longing]."[27] He goes on to point out that despite the widespread popularity of historical subjects and settings among readers, cinemagoers and television viewers, the concept of longing—particularly retrospective longing—was unfashionable in certain political and intellectual quarters, where it was regarded as

unhealthy and passive, as something defeatist which broadly speaking only befits a generation on the way out, and some other people with incurably conservative political opinions. It is the reactionaries who look back with longing, it is the reactionaries who with the useful aid of a selectively functioning memory persist in the idea of the good old times. And look at the expression "nostalgic," it is by now scarcely more than a term of abuse among intellectuals and book reviewers.[28]

The opening page of *A Love Story*, as already noted in our chapter 1, demonstrates the moral pressures exerted at this time on writers to cease dealing with "private" matters and to be "universal" in approach, with the narrator admitting that for a long time he had rejected the urge to write about himself and his brother until, finally, a decisive event in February 1970 made him change his mind. (With customary narrative dexterity, Evander does not reveal the nature of the event until the end of the book. It is, of course, Henning's suicide.) He decides to take the risk of being personal and telling about it, then quickly corrects his own terminology: " 'tell about' is in fact the wrong expression now I come to think about it, it's more a question of *providing an account . . .* of *recording the reality*" (11; my italics). A declared documentary intention provides a moral alibi for the handling of personal material. The problem can be highlighted with the aid of a brief quotation from a study of the literary scene of the period by a respected critic. He speaks of writers such as Göran Palm, Sven Lindqvist, and Björn Håkansson "attempting to break with an egocentric, personality centered view of life," and Håkansson's recent works are described as questioning "the very idea of personality itself, the assertion of selfhood, individualism, all typical features of traditional Western humanism."[29]

We may assume that Evander had struggled for some years with the problem of on the one hand sympathizing with politics which aid the growth of liberty, equality, and fraternity, while on the other feeling his freedom hampered by doctrinaire models. There are no overt polemics or apologetics in *A Love Story*—that is not his way— but when the politically suspect, reactionary notion of longing is shown to be indissolubly linked with the highly respectable term "commitment" or "involvement," we note a heretical synthesis at work. For Henning plans to write a love story which will also be about "unreserved commitment . . . it would illuminate the involvement that could save the world from destruction—yes, it would certainly be a very real Love Story" (124).

Elsewhere, Evander assumes that "no meaningful form of longing is entirely unrelated to anxiety," that at best this anxiety actually is able to "translate ambitions and feelings into action."[30] So the triad anxiety, longing, and commitment overlap and constitute the highly personal motor of creativity.

Postscript. As we have already noted, some critics reacted to Henning as though he had an identity in his own right and did not simply represent a complementary half of Per Gunnar. Others accepted the two brothers as symbolic complementary projections,[31] while a few spoke slightingly of there being something coquettish about Evander's playing with identities.[32] His reaction to the latter is illustrated by the following passage from his novel *Fear's Dwelling Place* (1980).

Some years ago I wrote a novel about the final period of Henning's life. Maybe it was a mistake to call the story a novel, I ought to have called it a report or documentary since it scarcely differed from reality.

But I wrote about Henning in order to try to get away from the time we spent together and in order to get it in perspective, as the saying goes.

I touched on the circumstances surrounding his suicide.

I described his fear and how he would wake at night and believe that his hands were turning into a bird's claws.

I tried as best I could to express his incurable longing and his violent aggression towards everything and everybody. . . . A number of reviewers in the daily press, including so-called authorial colleagues, proclaimed in their overbearing insolence that I had never had a brother.

According to them I was only engaged in mystification and playing with identities. . . . I pulled myself together . . . and wrote replies to two of the papers which had most obviously challenged my facts and most aggressively reproached me for bearing false witness. My rejoinder was returned by both papers with condescending letters asserting with icy arrogance that the matter was of no interest and that critics were immune from attack. . . .[33] I do not know what hurt me most in this whole affair.

That I was robbed of my own brother, to whom I had been so attached?

Or that I was considered incapable of something as elementary as the ability to provide a credible rendering of the truth?

I am damned if I know.

But the episode rooted in me a red-hot hatred of certain authors and critics in this country, a hatred which still today can make me shake with a primitive lust for revenge.

I little imagined then that the situation would be repeated a few years later.

This time it was not a question of Henning, it concerned a girl called Lillemor Holm.

But that is another story, and one I can hardly bring myself to think about any longer. (207-210)

The commotion surrounding *The Case of Lillemor Holm* will be discussed in chapter 4. Evander clearly finds the suggestion that he is not the sovereign arbiter of the veracity of his own fiction quite insupportable. The whole intricate question will be considered in chapter 6 of this study. Let us for the present examine how he tackles fiction and reality in his next novel.

The Story of Joseph

Berättelsen om Josef [The Story of Joseph, 1972] shows the author engaged on two separate assignments—the making of a television film and the writing of a novel, both of which feature a man who has killed his wife. The narrative does not present a continuous action— there are in fact four separate time schemes—but it reflects, fragmentarily, the various categories of material relating to the projected novel, as well as indicating the progress of the film. The data about the making of the film and the author's conditions of work, both cinematic and literary, appear to be entirely authentic. The "fiction" centers on the shift-worker Joseph, who after thirty-eight years in the iron foundry can no longer stand the pressures of night work, with disastrous results.[34] A wealth of material—which the author has divided and subdivided into Joseph's conditions of work, his home, personality, and family life, the "catastrophe," and letters from his daughter to the author—waits for the chosen opening image to spring to life, so that the story can be set in motion. The image is that of Joseph just off a train at the railway station of his home town, waiting uncertainly to see if his daughter will meet him. He feels a powerful, warm wind blowing round his heart, a sensation he later identifies as "anxiety." The narrator, meanwhile, is ensconced in a sandy hollow on a Swedish beach, surrounded by spiral-backed notebooks, muttering to himself: "I shall not leave this place until I can see the continuation and the pattern clearly" (12). But he mutters in vain, and a shower forces him to abandon his stand.

The television film which Evander is working on together with his colleague, Bengt Åke Kimbré, is based on a Swedish *cause célèbre* of 1889, known as the Yngsjö murder, in which a young bride was murdered and her husband and mother-in-law (additionally accused of having an incestuous relationship) were found guilty of the crime. The mother was the last woman to hang in Sweden, and her son, Per Nilsson, spent twenty-three years in prison before returning to his native parish, where his unfortunate wife's tombstone still bears the inscription: "In memory of Hanna Johansdotter born in North Björstorp on 3.13.1867. Murdered by her husband Per Nilsson and his mother in Yngsjö on 3.28.1889. The unhappy woman's prayers and tears moved them not one whit."

The film is to center on Per Nilsson's return after his years in prison, to show him visiting his wife's grave, and to suggest what may have filled his mind as he read the shocking epitaph—in short, to speculate about how he dealt with his sense of guilt. In this endeavor, Evander and his colleague were helped by an amazing chance discovery in an attic in the neighborhood, for what they came across was no less than a collection of notes written by Per Nilsson after his release from prison.

The reader can only gradually piece together the strands and elements of the text, but to give a straightforward summary, we find that Joseph Blomberg suddenly becomes sleepless at the age of fifty-eight and deteriorates so badly in health that he has to visit the works doctor, who gives him sleeping tablets. He improves marginally, but is soon sleepless again, and much against his will is transferred to less demanding work. Having pleaded in vain to return to his old job, he does the unheard-of thing of bursting into tears in the doctor's consulting room. He is put on sick-leave and more drugs. His depression and anxiety increase, but he is unable to explain his state of mind to his wife and daughter, as indeed he is powerless to account for it to himself. His helpless and baffled wife is too humble and unassuming to ring up the works' doctor or one of her husband's superiors, and Joseph starts drinking to steady his nerves. One day his daughter comes home to find her mother lying at the foot of the stairs and her father lying on his bed in a state of shock. Joseph's wife must have tried remonstrating with him in her simple, well-meaning way, provoking him in his drugged state to push her down the stairs. She never regains consciousness, and Joseph is charged with manslaughter and eventually sent to a psychiatric hospital for four years. The opening image of the book is in fact Joseph's return to his daughter's home after being discharged from the hospital.

Clearly there are some similarities but even greater differences between the respective situations of Per Nilsson the murderer, who is known to have been strengthened by faith in God's everlasting mercy, and the discharged Joseph, sedated and passive after his stretch in hospital, but still subject to recurrent bouts of fear, a man with an unresolved load of guilt and without the comfort of religious belief.

Per Nilsson's notes describe how he goes down to the sea on a winter's day and stands there praying for as long as he can withstand the icy blast: "I thanked Him for my long, rich life, I thanked Him for forgiving me my sins each day, I thanked Him for the landscape in which I had the good fortune to grow up, I thanked Him, equally, for the fury of the sea and that He forgave mankind's unpremeditated actions" (195). Joseph, on the other hand, sits at his daughter's kitchen table with a sheet of paper in front of him divided into two columns headed respectively "People I have harmed" and "People who have harmed me." In the former (left-hand) column there was "a total of some twenty names. In the right-hand column there was only one name, but it had been crossed out heavily" (206). Seeing it, his daughter "burst into tears in her room and lay thinking of the deceptive sense of security surrounding him, a security which was

nothing more than a large and fragile sack of anxiety and memories"
(206).

Thematization of guilt and fear. The narrator widens the
scope of the concept of guilt by asking rhetorically what epitaphs could
possibly do justice to the holocaust of the month in which he is
writing: to the daily deaths of women and children in Vietnam, the
young victims of violence in Londonderry, earthquakes in Chile and
Argentina, air disasters and "mercy killings." The list is endless, as is
the sum of human suffering. The wider perspective, it is tempting to
believe, is introduced by Evander to show—if it should be needed—
that he is aware of the global perspective, while his observation that
"the number of people killed and the distance to the disaster area
stand in inverse proportion to the human ability to feel involved"
(137), appears to justify him in writing about one aging foundry
worker.

It may be a covert example of the problem of guilt thematized in a
highly personal way when the narrator recalls a walk he took with
Joseph's daughter Ingrid, during the course of which she calls out a
proposal of marriage to him across a lake. He pretends not to hear and
refuses to be drawn when she repeats it, and when the girl reaches
him, he accidentally strikes her on the face as he lurches sideways, a
blow which evidently causes her considerable pain, but for which he
never apologizes. Now the man who is afraid of emotional involvement
is a familiar Evander phenomenon, and it is tempting to regard the
incident by the lake as a miniature variation on the main theme of
inflicting bodily harm on someone dear to us, involuntarily yet in the
Freudian sense subconsciously motivated. The Yngsjö murderer
claimed to have been innocent of the murder of his wife but admitted
to having "sinned in thought" (196), and Joseph, befuddled by
sedatives, clearly felt an aggressive impulse toward his wife, as did the
narrator toward Ingrid when she broached the subject of marriage. It
would be possible to argue that the narrator at some deep level fears
the emotional involvement of marriage. His minor violence serves to
ward off the dangers of greater violence within marriage, such as that
exhibited by Nilsson and Joseph.

An undeniable thematization is that of the link between fear and
guilt. On the level of individuals, we are told that a frightened boxer
is a dangerous man—his fear makes him erratic and undependable,

and likely to hurt his opponent. And as for the collective, societal level, the narrator refers to the anxiety endured by its weaker members: "How much work has not been carried out under threats and intimidation, how many feats and trials of strength at work have not had fear as their ultimate precondition . . . a fear which undeniably has helped to increase production . . . a fear which satisfies managements' demands for increased profits" (113). Joseph's tragedy can be traced back to his fear of redundancy and worthlessness, for he is a mere worker whose anxiety symptoms are not taken seriously and he ends up by killing his wife. Evander shows us his daughter Ingrid, who has trained as a teacher and moved outside her parents' environment, scarcely able to handle all the hatred and anger she feels toward the works' management for a state of affairs in which it is still regarded as perfectly normal for a desperate wife not to dare to turn to anyone for help.

The novel speaks of people who have been taught to hide their feelings and shoulder their "slave role" (94). This may be emotive language, but the quiet insistence with which facts are laid before the reader seems to warrant it. Medical investigations show that every second-shift worker in heavy industry suffers from stomach and sleep problems, yet the industry and its medical advisors have done nothing to counteract these effects. Furthermore, the majority of the workers are unswervingly loyal to their employers and mates, questioning neither the shift system nor the strain involved in working with the intense heat of furnaces and molten metal, when the slightest slip or momentary inattention has fatal consequences. They recognize only the validity of bodily injuries or illnesses such as ulcers, broken bones, and burns, but suspect bad backs and altogether reject nervous troubles where they themselves are concerned, regarding emotional or psycho-somatic disorders as an upper-class indulgence.

The poet Stig Sjödin (see chapter 1) provides the novel with a prefatory poem, which crystallizes Joseph's situation when his strong physique finally lets him down, and he is gripped by shame and fear. It ends: "Consumption is okay, like ulcers and blood pressure./ But heaven preserve the man whose mind starts to crack,/ and who wanders sleepless every hour of the twenty-four./ They hang a warning bell on him."

The fact that there is a class dimension to the problem is reinforced by the following juxtapositions: media man Evander and colleagues regard September as a good month, for the rich variety of summer being over, their appetite for work is sharp and stimulated. For Joseph, the best time of the year was the middle of winter when the night shift could open the narrow windows near the furnaces and let the cold come flooding in. The snow-laden air smelt like sweet perfume and brought intense bodily well-being. But the pleasure had to be paid for with colds and rheumatism. The process of aging has different implications, too, for the two classes. The worker has to be on guard against greying hair and missing teeth, those outward signs of age, for the specter of redundancy lurks around the corner for the man suspected of not being able to keep up with the pace and demands of his job. Set against this, we find a vignette of the narrator having a lunch date with an ex-girlfriend, who remarks cattily that he has gone grey at the temples, an observation he counters smoothly, and the sole consequence of which is wounded male pride, when he confirms its accuracy in front of the washroom mirror after good-byes.

The metanovel.   Evander was not alone in opening the eyes of middle-class readers to the everyday reality of fellow human beings hitherto assumed to be adequately catered for in terms of industrial health. Already in 1970, Maja Ekelöf had described her life as an office cleaner in *Rapport från en skurhink* [Report from a scrubbing bucket], and 1972, the year of publication of *The Story of Joseph*, saw the simultaneous publication of Göran Palm's *Ett år på LM* [A Year at LM Ericsson], Sture Källberg's *Ackord* [Piece work] and Marit Paulsen's *Du människa!* [You, A Human Being!]. But whereas these last three are overtly political, Evander's book represents an ambitious attempt to produce an intricate literary artifact as well as an exposure of poor pay and shift work as an effective means of oppression.

At the same time, it cannot be denied that there is a problem with a novel in which the narrator explicitly and repeatedly claims to be getting bogged down. Two hypotheses suggest themselves. He may be showing us that his creativity is being blocked by the large amount of documentary material stacked on his desk, as well as by his determination not to become emotionally involved in the case, i.e., he may be demonstrating in concrete terms the hampering effect of the prescriptive literary-ideological climate obtaining at the time. Alternatively, focusing in his text on the actual writing of this novel may be an alienatory device on Evander's part, a Brechtian *Verfremdung* designed to activate his readers' intellectual awareness, and force them to face the plight of the weak and acquiescent victims of an industrial society. But if alienation were the object of the exercise, the novel would be based on a contrivance, for the author's claimed inability to write his novel would then be the cornerstone upon which it is actually built, so that the state of affairs he overtly deplores in fact is essential to his purposes.

This rather convoluted reasoning can in itself perhaps be taken as proof that the element of ambiguity and mystery so characteristic of Evander occasionally unsettles his readers. An extreme example of this reaction was offered by a fellow writer who spoke of his getting tied up in linguistic ironies and literary pirouettes,[35] but he was roundly rebuked by another, weighty colleague, who commended Evander's ability, by means of various distancing devices, to keep his reader cool, aware, and analytical in relation to the social panorama which he paints in book after book.[36] The Swedish Academy, for its part, thought so highly of *The Story of Joseph* that it bestowed the Zorn literary prize on its author.[37]

Evander himself went on record in 1976 as saying that he considered the book to be his best. It is also clear that what pleased him most was when ordinary readers wrote to him about its *matter*, and what pleased him least was reviewers' tendency to focus attention on its *form*. It brings to an end the series of books, starting with *Close Relations*, in which he experiments with a variety of formal techniques. What might be called his era of realism is about to begin.

Chapter Four

Popular Success

The Last Adventure

After the disappointment of having sold not more than six hundred copies of what he regarded as his best book,[1] *The Story of Joseph,* the culmination in his view of seven years of novel writing, Evander determined to try to reach a wider public. He embarked on the first of a series of broad, realistic narratives, centering on a main character for whom he shows undisguised sympathy. Detachment, distancing effects, and the presence of an objectified narrator called "Per Gunnar Evander" are exchanged for straight narration by an invisible author.[2] It proved to be the breakthrough he had been waiting for.

Det sista äventyret [The Last Adventure, 1973] features the classic situation of a young man dogged by a dominating and overprotective mother, much given to weeping whenever her son proves a disappointment to her—a frequent occurrence—and declaring that it is fortunate that his father has not lived to see the day. He finds himself steamrollered into an engagement with a sensible and stable nurse, who thinks there are more important values in life than sex, and who has a cosy relationship with her prospective mother-in-law; the two women vie with one another in washing his socks and underpants and in admonishing him to eat up, and to be careful and hardworking.

This rather overweight and bespectacled antihero is known as Jimmy to everyone except his mother, who insists on using his baptismal names Karl-Erik. He has experienced a series of failures: he left school without matriculating, his period of conscription came to a precipitate and inglorious end, and he returned to civilian life without qualifications or a job. He is then offered temporary work as a biology teacher at the local high school (biology and nature study being his passion), and once there he is bowled over by a beautiful sixteen-year-old pupil, Helfrid, with an uncomplicated and direct approach to sex. She seduces him the very first time they are alone together, in a way which he had thought was reserved for gentlemen's magazines. Jimmy cannot bring himself to tell Helfrid of his engagement, nor does he break it off; instead, he dreams of his fiancée breaking it off, for he cannot bear to hurt anyone—particularly not someone who, along with his mother, has done so much for him. He is besotted by Helfrid, although aware of the fact that they have no real interests in common, apart from the immediate pleasure of their relationship. He is violently jealous of any other presumptive boy friend of hers, not without reason as it subsequently transpires. The untenable situation leads swiftly to catastrophe: first, his fiancée discovers them together in a state of undress and breaks with him, not long afterward Jimmy out of impotent jealousy is driven to striking Helfrid, his temporary job is terminated (due to complaints about his relationship with a pupil), and overwhelmed by feelings of guilt and failure, he imagines that he is going blind as a punishment. One night he breaks into an optician's and runs amok there until the police arrive. He wakes up in a mental hospital.

The second half of the book shows us Jimmy's gradual recovery. For some considerable time yet, he imagines he will go blind at any moment and that shoals of sticklebacks are heading straight for his eyes in order to devour them. His mother visits him and asks weepingly if he realizes how he has disgraced her by getting himself arrested and ending up in a *mental* hospital? Gradually, Jimmy establishes rapport with one of the psychiatrists, and in company with five other patients he spends six months at an experimental therapeutic community in a country house, where medication is largely replaced by therapy. When the novel ends, Jimmy is some way along the road to recovery.

The psychological perspective. *The Last Adventure* differs from Evander's preceding novels in that it puts before the reader material directly reflecting the main character's emotions and inner life. We recognize a new will on his part to demonstrate cause and effect in psychological terms. This does not mean, however, that the narrator provides any overt explanations. The dramatist in Evander favors the implicit as opposed to the explicit, and makes extensive use of dialogue. And just as a playwright does not comment on and explain the dramatic action of his plays except through the words of his characters, so readers of *The Last Adventure* have to make their own connections within the text without prompting from the narrator. But the clues are plentiful. They have to perceive that Jimmy's overwhelming fear of going blind is explained when he tells the psychiatrist about his mother nagging him as a child to take care not to break his spectacles, how his spectacles used to get misted over because she always forced extra woollies on him, and how she used to punish the short-sighted Jimmy by removing his spectacles when he had been naughty. It is clear that until he can free himself from her domination, he will continue to react in an infantile way. Going berserk in the optician's must have been a desperate protest, which fortunately landed him in hospital rather than in prison.

Like most emotionally disturbed people, Jimmy is painfully resistant to delving into the roots of his problem. When the psychiatrist asks him at the end of the book if he would still define *angst*—the nameless fear which grips him—as ice in the throat (which he had done on arrival at the hospital), Jimmy assents and is told that he is improving, but still has a long way to go. It seems fair to deduce that a patient who defines *angst* in terms of its symptoms still has a lot of self-analysis left to do.

Certain of Jimmy's psychological mechanisms are absolutely clear and are illustrated in a series of dramatic episodes—it is not coincidence that the novel was turned into a successful film. An early scene is taken from Jimmy's period of national service; with a group of friends he has decided always to salute a lamppost in the barrack square as a symbolic protest against the futility of army life. When members of the group gradually disperse, he feels that the rest of the chaps in his plutoon expect him to carry on alone, particularly since the authorities now have their disapproving eyes on him. In much the same compulsive way, he feels obliged to heave a radio out of the window of their fifth-floor quarters when a record request show plays a particularly sentimental evergreen, since he had rashly vowed to react in this way if it should turn out to be the next record. In deep disgrace, he drops his loaded lunch tray smack on the cafeteria floor twice running under the baleful eye of the duty officer. On one level he desperately wants to stay out of trouble and gain the approval of authority, at a deeper level he wants to protest, and it is always the deeper level which ultimately proves the strongest—the unresolved conflict with his mother is the paradigm for all his relations with superiors.

The threat of the opposite sex. The roles played by men and women in Jimmy's life differ significantly. His mother has been the destructive force in his life (his shadowy father died relatively early), and his fiancée is an extension of her. The libidinous Helfrid releases some of his inhibitions, but ultimately she, too, has a destructive effect on him, for he cannot handle his sexual insecurity and jealousy. On the other hand, Jimmy recovers with the help of a male psychiatrist, and some of his happiest hours in the therapeutic community are spent on rowing expeditions with Bruno, a male fellow patient. The shy and reticent Bruno tells him that these bird-watching expeditions on the lake are like adventures for him, with something new and unexpected happening each time, at which Jimmy "felt a surge of warmth suffusing his body, and suddenly could not see how he could ever become depressed again, how sorrow could ever take root in him again. What Bruno had just said was one of the nicest things anyone had ever said to him" (238). After a particularly long and successful expedition, which in fact proves to be their last one, Bruno—who has an ineradicable death wish—takes an overdose. The novel's title, *The Last Adventure*, would seem to refer to this particular expedition of theirs, but the inner logic of the story seems to be the unfolding of a series of "adventures" undergone by Jimmy; first, the tragicomical adventures of his army career, then the equally tragicomical episodes of his clandestine affair with Helfrid, and finally the adventure of his nervous breakdown and slow recovery. Seen in this light, his last adventure leads him toward accepting his true self and overcoming his feelings of guilt and inadequacy. It is in relation to *men*, however, that Jimmy succeeds in proving and reassuring himself. A central episode in this respect finds him standing in the barrack square surveying the damage done by the heavy radio he heaved out of the fifth-floor window; he waits for retribution to overtake him, his throat turns to ice, and a single tone, as though from a tuning fork, reverberates in his chest—two physical symptoms of extreme fear. But his fellow conscripts crowd noisily round him, showing their approval of his action, whereupon the "ice" melts and he feels suffused with warmth and security. This same scene is recalled on the book's final page, shortly after Jimmy has told the psychiatrist that his acute anxiety symptoms are fading and that he wonders if perhaps it is God who has helped him. Let us at this point remember that God is the ultimate Father figure, the Transcendental Male, and then watch Jimmy lie down on a sunlit wooden jetty by the lakeside, placing his spectacles beside him *without first having carried out his habitual obsessive act of rubbing them:*

He fell asleep although he always found it so difficult to sleep in direct sunlight, and he continued to lie there sleeping at the far end of the jetty . . . with his glasses beside him. He slept quite a long time.

And in his dream the boys returned to him, one after one, or in groups of three or four. They just came to him and it was that bright, dusty day in the barrack square, they came and pressed closed to him and it reminded him of when it got hot in the tent because they had heated it too much, they were loud and noisy like real rough guys, and they boxed him loosely in the stomach and chest.

Bully to you, Jimmy boy, they said. That wasn't half bad!

And it was light and warm and the air was full of dry dust which seemed to have settled in compact clouds over the whole barrack square.

Bully to you, Jimmy boy, they said again as the ring closed tighter and tighter round him.

He was prepared to bet that almost every single one of them had come down to the square. (287)

Mondays with Fanny

The Last Adventure was the first book of what Evander called "a trilogy about how we are marked and molded during the earliest years of our lives."[3] In the second, *Måndagarna med Fanny* [Mondays with Fanny, 1974], the main character works in the damp basement storeroom of a firm of plumbers, where he and his poorly paid mates act as buffers between management and the men who go out and do the work. It is not a promising literary environment, but Evander's sympathy for his characters imbues their awkward pauses and trivial exchanges with real warmth. The citation for the Big Novel Prize awarded him for *Mondays with Fanny* notes that in it, he "once again, with realism, imagination, and tenderness presents a picture of Swedish everyday life, emphasizing inhibited human relationships and the possibilities of release which love can provide."[4]

The novel opens with a hatless and coatless man walking unsteadily along a wintry road into town. This is Robert Erikson, suffering from a severe hangover and recently roped in to search for an elderly woman who has inexplicably disappeared from the car in which her son left her alone for a few moments. Far from helping, however, Robert proves a decided nuisance and is dumped by the roadside. He staggers home and slumps dispiritedly over the kitchen table, drinking beer and nursing a headache. He is married to a previously widowed schoolteacher, and they are childless. His wife, Gudrun, never challenges him outright about his drinking, but just drops discreet hints and reproaches, while he sometimes secretly wishes she would tell him off instead. Altogether, what he tends to wish she would do are things which she can have no notion of, because he never tells her what he really feels. Since childhood, he has been taught "to swallow joy, sorrow, and anger . . . has learned from the word go, that self-control is the jewel among virtues" (214).

Robert's widower father, a retired schoolmaster, is seriously ill in hospital with pulmonary emphysema, from which he is slowly choking to death. Robert gets time off from work to visit him on Monday afternoons, and one day he gives a lift to a young nurse, Fanny, whose spontaneous warmth and friendliness disarm him. When he runs into her on a subsequent visit, he cannot bring himself to tell her that he is married. In his happy incredulity that so positive a relationship has arisen between them, he shelves the necessity for openness. His frozen emotional resources start to thaw out, and they spend some happy Monday afternoons together in a friend's cottage until Fanny, inevitably, learns that Robert has lied to her. When she no longer wishes to go on meeting him, Robert cannot contain his misery and drives out to the empty cottage, which he despairingly vandalizes with an ax. On returning home, he lays his head in his wife's lap and weeps for the first time in his adult life. She rocks him in her arms and whispers that she is there, and that she knows how much it hurts to lose someone you love. The fact that she thinks he is mourning his father, who has just died, does not detract from the genuine contact which has been established between them.

Relations between father and son. Robert's relationship with Fanny forms one strand of this novel, his relationship with his father another, and together they constitute the threads with which a picture of love, active or inhibited, proffered or withheld, is woven. In many senses, Robert is a *failure*. He has not lived up to his father's expectations. Whereas his younger brother has become an engineer and is a credit to his father, Robert has a menial job, and ekes out his wages by working part-time as a cinema attendant in the evenings. His father corrects his grammar and bad language. When Robert is under the influence of drink he calls his father "pa," which the old man regards as uncultivated. On one such occasion, he suddenly confides in his father that ever since childhood he has wondered why he once hit him across the face when he asked about a sexual matter, instead of answering the question. His father claims to have no recollection of the incident, but his son persists:

> Just wham! and then there was nothing for it, but to scram off like some bloody dog.
> Mind your language, Robert!
> It's not a question of language now, pa! (84)

The old man is incapable of offering an explanation, and instead he has a severe attack of breathlessness. But although he drops his inhaler, Robert stands rooted to the floor, unable to bring himself to pick it up.

His stored-up resentment manifests itself in a variety of similar ways, as does the fact that his father himself had a difficult childhood. In fact, it is Evander's achievement to demonstrate for us the sad irony of two products of parental oppression, both angry with each other and equally victims of their upbringing. In one way, Robert resembles the father he criticizes: the exasperated hospital staff observe that old Mr. Erikson is obstinate, and so is Robert. When the old man asks regretfully why it all (meaning life) has to end with his even lacking the strength to walk across to the window, his son replies:

> But you know what it's all due to. This isn't something which has come out of the blue.
> Nobody knows what it's due to.
> Why must you be so obstinate, father. It's due to the fact that you've smoked too much, that you didn't give it up in time. You know that as well as I do. (126)

What Robert does not admit is that a good many of his own social and health problems stem from too much drinking.

When Robert challenges his father about bygone injustices, his father counters by saying that Robert has always been ungrateful for the chances he was given: "Sigvard [his brother] was appreciative, which you never were, Robert!" (120). Their exchanges highlight the fact that the human memory functions selectively and represses unwanted items. The old man recalls a classroom incident when a boy claimed that foxes in the north of Sweden are bigger than those in the south, and another boy backed him up by asserting that German foxes are even smaller, and they get progessively smaller the further south you go (104). When Robert's father cast doubt on the validity of this, young Robert put up his hand and pointed out that it must be true, since there are no foxes at all in Africa (105). The odd thing is that Mr. Erikson now recounts the story with evident pleasure in his son's powers of deduction, whereas Robert asks bitterly why he was thrown out of the classroom.

Why on earth would I have wanted to throw you out?
I suppose you thought it got too noisy in the classroom with everybody laughing. (106)

A silence falls between them, which his father breaks by observing that Robert only remembers negative things from his schooldays, adding that his brother Sigvard does the very opposite, but then Robert flunked out of high school, "and so there probably isn't very much that's pleasant to remember" (107). The reader tends to believe in the validity of Robert's recollections as opposed to his father's, but Evander undermines our belief in his infallibility by subsequently showing us the two men having a disagreement about a sporting record when Robert—dead certain that he knows best—gets the dates wrong. The unspoken truth Evander thereby conveys is that, irrespective of whose recollections are objectively speaking most accurate, what matters to the individual is how he *feels* about the situation.

The old man's health deteriorates sharply toward the end, and he laments that life is such a miserable business. When Robert says: "Don't you think, all the same, that there's some happiness in the

world, somewhere, pa?'' the answer comes back sharply: "Don't call
me pa!'' (247). Not until his father is finally laid out on a slab in the
mortuary, does Robert stroke his cheek, but as he tells his workmates,
"at the same time I knew it was too late, however bloody much I
stood there patting him. Because when he was alive there wasn't much
of that, there didn't seem to be time for it somehow. . ." (272).

The love story in this book is just as much about the yearning of the
child within the forty-two-year-old man for his father's approval, as it
is about an encounter between a man and a woman. In spite of the old
man's bickering and the younger man's truculence, it is clear that at a
very deep level they are stretching out their hands toward each other.

Relationship between mother and son.   Although it is Robert's
relationship to his father that is demonstrated at length, his relationship to his mother is, in its way, equally problematic. Fifteen years
after her death, he can still be gripped by a sudden conviction that she
is passing by in the street above the basement storeroom where he
works:

> he has to hurry up the stairs out into the street to check on it. Although he
> mostly stops when he reaches the last step and stands there a while, looking
> down the street towards the station.
> But no Ma Elin has passed by, she has been dead for fifteen years, and as
> Robert stands there on the top step, looking around him, his fear generally
> turns into an indefinable sense of shame. He cannot understand how he can
> be so daft each time, but the conviction is so strong that he could bet on the
> fact that she had just gone by. (78–79)

A childhood memory is linked to these episodes: his mother left a
shop without him in order to teach him a lesson. Thirty-seven years
later, the fear associated with being abandoned wells irresistibly up. It
is symptomatic of Robert's psychological makeup that he has never
mentioned these anxiety states to anyone, and he is so little given to
introspection, that he is probably unaware of the link which the author
clearly demonstrates between his chronic stomach pains and his habit
of repressing spontaneous expressions of emotion.

Robert's passivity.   One of Robert's striking characteristics is his
passivity and his unwillingness to take initiatives—he even shirks the
simple task of speaking to the staff nurse of his father's ward and lets

his wife do it instead. In fact, the only spontaneity Robert evinces is of an aggressive kind when he is drunk; in this state, he subjects the projectionist at the cinema from which he, Robert, has been sacked, to a violent beating, and after Fanny's break with him, he goes berserk in the cottage where they used to meet. When sober, he waits for other people to act first, which is precisely what Fanny does, and she even succeeds in compelling him to meet her halfway. We may recall that Helfrid bowled over the uncertain, self-doubting Jimmy (in *The Last Adventure*) and momentarily liberated him sexually, but that their incompatibility in other respects brought their affair to a violent end. Fanny's influence on Robert is far more benign that Helfrid's on Jimmy. In fact, for the first time in an Evander novel, we meet a woman who is wholly a power for good.

Robert has the greatest difficulty in showing what he feels. When for instance, his wife goes on a week's skiing holiday, he feels lost and restless, and after she has rung off from a telephone call, he feels dejected, wishing that she had asked him if he felt lonely—except, of course, that he has never told her how lonely he does feel when she is away. After her return, he creeps into her bed and they make love briefly and unsuccessfully, and he then lies awake wondering whether he is getting impotent, whether she does not excite him any longer, or whether he does not excite her and she only agrees to make love in order to avoid painful explanations. Perhaps she is thinking of her first husband? Ideas and questions buzz through his mind, but he does not utter a word about them to her, he "swallows" them. He never tells her how often he wishes that she would take the amorous initiative.

What Fanny does is to show Robert that he is worth loving, and that mutual trust and spontaneity are possible—even if they only last a very short time in their particular relationship. In the final scene, when Robert lies with his head in his wife's lap, shaking with sobs and a feeling of hopelessness, he simultaneously feels an infinite sense of relief. Crying is another way of saying something. Communication has been established between them.

The theme of loss. If we stop to think about various episodes scattered through the book, it is possible to see them as variations on the theme of loss. There is the elderly mother who unaccountably vanishes from her son's car, and who, although reference is made to her at intervals, never reappears. There is Robert, down in the basement, feeling a sudden contraction of the heart because he thinks his dead mother is passing by in the street above. As a boy, Robert was given a pair of exceptionally fine gloves for Christmas, one of which he almost immediately loses, to his parents' fury, and for which he goes on searching in vain for years: "he never found it, but neither did he ever give up hope that he would" (263). A further loss is that of Robert's father, and the text supports the sense of concrete bereavement when Fanny asks Robert what it feels like after his father's death and he answers: "That pa disappeared, you mean?" (268). Finally, there is the loss of Fanny herself.

There are no overt links between these elements, and indeed some readers have felt dissatisfaction with the unresolved mystery of the disappearing mother in the car, because they have taken it at face value. But, of course, it is safe to say that nothing should ever be taken at face value in the work of a serious novelist. Since it is overwhelmingly clear that Robert's lack of success and self-confidence has its roots in his upbringing, and since the only thing we are told about his relationship to his mother is the episode when she withdraws her presence from him, it is not hard to divine that the missing mother in the car is symbolic of absent maternal love.[5] By the same token, his continued search for the missing glove is a symbolic manifestation of his sense of loss. But the novel ends in hope, when loss is exchanged for gain—when repressed misery gives way to mutuality—as Robert dares to express his pain.

Fanny herself.   One reviewer was so captivated by Fanny that he regretted that she merely had the role of "the man's rib, a parenthesis in Robert's recovery."[6] He continued:

> Evander's next book ought probably not to be about a man with nervous problems, who is finally healed. Because here [is] . . . a magnificent portrait of a woman. There is a charm in Fanny's dialogue, a cheerful exuberance at once girlish and maternal, above all there is a stream of goodness in the way she takes on Robert, a goodness which oddly enough seems entirely credible. . . .
>
> Vilhelm Moberg and Lars Ahlin are men, but they have given us finer portraits of women than any women authors could do. Per Gunnar Evander has a natural place in the line of such men. We need to meet a woman like

Fanny in a full-length portrait, not just as an interlude on Mondays, not merely as a stage in a man's progress towards maturity.[7]

But well-meaning suggestions from reviewers are like dragonflies darting across the surface of deep waters. They can scarcely affect the depths from which creativity wells up. Evander was not primarily concerned with harmonious and good people, he was engaged in charting the progress of human beings at a painful remove from Fanny's warm spontaneity. So he continued, in his next book, to focus on a "man with nervous problems," with two women in ancillary roles representing successive stages in his "progress toward maturity."

Earth Divine

Härlig är jorden [Earth Divine, 1975] is also a novel about living through a crisis and coming to terms with bereavement (in the widest sense). It opens with the first-person narrator, Richard Hansson, watching the departure of his girl friend Harriet, who has been living with him for the past seven months and eleven days. The exactitude of the chronological calculation must be a measure of his grief, but he resolutely refuses to admit the pain he feels—either to himself or to anyone else. He sometimes snuggles down into Harriet's empty bed, but *without thinking about her*, as he points out to himself. He claims not to miss her, but somewhere, uneasily, he is aware of repressing thoughts and memories with which he might be unable to cope. In short, he "organizes" his emotions, just as he did when, as a teenager, he lost both parents through drowning. "I somehow succeeded in deriving a certain comfort from the fact that they [my parents] had been spared serious illnesses and protracted death-throes. I was strong enough to organize my feelings—I can't explain it in any other way— I was able to rationalize with the crazy logic enshrined in the phrase 'probably all for the best" (20). It was not until several years after the disaster that he began to be haunted by memories and dreams of them, in which the family was happily united but under threat of some nebulous danger.

Richard teaches science subjects at a folk high school. He is aware that his students regard him as provocatively detached at times, yet he fails to see the humor of a caricature of himself in their house magazine, with a text-balloon reading: "Everyone says that I don't care about anything, but I don't give a damn about that" (39). He has been brought up in a home where ambition and a sense of duty were paramount virtues. His N.C.O. father had a military bark even when speaking about the weather, and Richard reacted by developing a fundamental prejudice against everyone in uniform of any kind. Despite this, his students have wagered among themselves that he must be a reservist. In this respect, the father-son paradigm resembles that in *Mondays with Fanny*, where problems connected with self-control and repression are also passed down from parent to child.

Richard starts suffering from insomnia and blinding headaches, with a band of pain drawn tightly round his skull. Despising all forms of abnormality and illness, he finds his predicament acutely humiliating, particularly when it becomes clear to both students and staff that he is in no state to function normally. He rebukes the students time after time for the slightest thing—while simultaneously observing his own irrational behavior with contempt and loathing: "I hated myself, I wished myself the worst of everything in the world" (199). His misery is compounded by guilt feelings, yet he persists with his wrongheadedness.

The only person Richard can relax with, when he is at his worst, is a down-and-out ex-lumberjack, who sells him homedistilled liquor. He consistently rebuffs a warm-hearted and motherly colleague who tries to draw him out by speaking of Harriet. This wise and kindly woman, several years his senior, has been through a painful divorce herself, and it is greatly thanks to her persistence—despite his rudeness—that he finally pulls out of his crisis.

Another friend in need is the school doctor, who senses that more than trivial headache symptoms are at stake, and persuades him to come for a drive:

By the way, you're living on your own now, aren't you?
What makes you ask?. . . . It's not her [Harriet] that's giving me a headache, if that's what you think! . . .
You're not by any chance going round wishing that things will come right again between you?
Of course not! . . .

I mean, maybe it was you who wanted her to move?
Well, I suppose it was both of us.
So she didn't leave without your wanting her to?
What do you mean?
I mean, it wasn't her who deserted you? . . .
Can't you shut up! Can't you stop jawing about that bloody bitch who has nothing whatever to do with this! Can't you bloody well shut up, shut up, shut up! (114–117)

Richard beats his fists against the dashboard of the stationary car, then hides his face in his hands and starts sobbing. Later, he grudgingly admits that there were odd moments when he and Harriet were happy together, for instance the three months when Harriet was expecting a baby. In fact, this was a period when he went round with a feeling of indefinable joy spreading throughout his arteries and suffusing his whole body, but he scarcely mentioned this feeling to her, because he felt embarrassed, having no idea that a man could feel that he, too, was expecting a baby. When Victoria, the motherly colleague, taxes him with not-admitting how greatly he longs for and misses Harriet, and explains to him what a failure Harriet had felt after her miscarriage, Richard answers that he was delighted about her pregnancy.

Did you tell her so?
Tell her and tell her! She sure must have noticed that I was pleased.
Is it so sure?
Do I have to beetle round babbling about everything I feel?
If you want my opinion, Richard, that's exactly what you need to do. (160)

In the end, Richard starts dreaming of Harriet and reaches the point when he can admit his desperate longing. He writes to her and suggests a meeting. Although she never turns up, the very act of making the move helps his recovery. On returning to the school from the abortive meeting, he runs into a young assistant matron and actually asks her to go for a walk with him a few days later. He starts sleeping without tablets.
As Richard sets off for a solitary walk one morning, he hears students singing a hymn, *Earth Divine*, which he remembers from his

parents' funeral. The countryside suddenly springs to life again for him and appears unbelievably beautiful. This experience is repeated not long afterward, filling him with a sense of well-being reminiscent of the time when Harriet's baby was expected. He catches sight of the assistant matron as he walks across the hills, and they approach each other laughing happily, which is the point at which the book ends.

Thematization: The womb. Schematically, the novel's development can be seen as proceeding from repression to crisis to turning point to recovery. The repressive tendency has its genesis in Richard's upbringing in an overambitious home, and leads to his unsatisfactory relationship with Harriet, toward whom he fails to be loving and open. The crisis is precipitated by Harriet's departure—inevitable, sooner or later—and runs a severe course, threatening to put him in hospital. Thanks, above all, to the helpfulness of Victoria and the doctor, a turning point is reached when Richard is gradually prevailed upon both to talk and think about Harriet. It is a measure of his emotional liberation and recovery that he has the urge to make contact with the assistant matron.

There are two motifs of central significance to Richard's situation. When this seemingly unfeeling man with the stiff upper lip is plagued by an iron band of pain round his skull, it is a fantasy which appears to be connected with the security of the womb which comforts him. He tries to keep the pain (in itself an obvious symptom of repression since talking of Harriet gives him "a pain in the nut," [179]) at bay by lying on his bed in a fetal position, staring at a lighted candle, and recalling a scene from his early childhood. It is a skating expedition with mother and father, uncles, an aunt, cousins, all moving in unison across the ice, he himself being the smallest and weakest of them, yet none of them speed away and leave him: "I was one of them all, because no one had yet left the group and moved away from me" (131). This fantasy is all the more illuminating for showing us the child behind the controlled facade of the grown man. Evander has privately explained that the reason Richard has such a particularly difficult time and such severe symptoms is that he is so rigid and so sternly disciplined.[8] Yet when nothing else helps, this memory of childhood security functions as a talismanic device for staving off the onslaught of pain. Ultimately, as the weeks go by, this reversion to an infantile state fails to have the desired effect, for when Richard resorts to the fetal position, the hitherto repressed image of Harriet obtrudes itself between him and his comforting vision, forcing him back into the adult world.

A related motif, representing happiness and a sense of inner well-being, derives from memories of the time when he was an expectant father. This state becomes linked to the hymn, *Earth Divine*, which was played at his parents' funeral. For as Richard, on the road to recovery, rediscovers the beauty of nature, so he hums the hymn and recalls the joy he felt over his unborn child. There is a circularity between the memory of being with his parents on the ice and the joy of expecting his own child, a circularity which redeems the traumatic loss of father and mother by drowning. It must surely be the case that the new love relationship, which seems to be opening up for Richard at the end of the book, is not a banal happy end, but rather a demonstration of the way in which the human psyche—at a profound elemental level—derives comfort from the merciful cycle of nature, which allows generation to succeed generation, and life to succeed death. A child can, after all, be said to be both physically generated by and spiritually regenerative of its parents.

Thematization: Accepting loss. It is obvious that what is placed before us in this book is a man who desperately resists facing his own emotional pain—he drives it underground, whence it returns with redoubled fury as physical pain. It would seem that the theme of allowing pain to surface is varied in small episodes. Early on in the book, a neighboring farmer's wife asks Richard to shoot her husband's faithful old hunting dog, since he himself cannot bring himself to do it. When Richard arrives to carry out the request, the farmer has already, with infinite pain, killed his old friend and has drunk himself into a stupor. Richard is shaken, and returns to the school, tense and upset, but unable to suggest why the incident should have affected him so deeply. The reader can conjecture that the farmer's willingness to face bereavement—and his deep distress at having done so—is a challenge to Richard to do the same: to face his loss and the pain it entails.

Nor is it probably coincidental that the disabled ex-lumberjack, Oscar, confides in Richard that he is a homosexual—a lonely and vulnerable situation—at the very point when Richard himself is reaching the stage of allowing his own emotional pain to surface. We could go further, and see Richard's persistence in letting Oscar think that he may well accompany him on a visit to Denmark, despite his own awareness that he will do nothing of the kind, as a form of desertion or abandonment—an acting out of what he himself has been subjected to. By the same token, an incident when Richard is instrumental in helping Victoria's son, on the run from the police after an episode of violence, to give himself up and face the loss of his freedom, can be read as another variation on the theme of facing reality.

Criticisms. When *Dagens Nyheter* arranged a symposium with ten of its journalists to discuss the book, the participants' readings were strikingly divided.[9] Some of them found the themes and their treatment banal, others were absorbed by Richard's crisis. Disagreement centered on the author's relationship to his alter ego, and whether or not his text could be read as a critique of Richard's attitudes and values. Some participants found Evander's controlled prose an inadequate vehicle for a *retrospective* account of a crisis of repression, from which the narrator had successfully emerged. Both admirers and detractors were agreed, however, that the novel was not one of Evander's best, and that "he ought to spend more time on the next one."

With regard to the question of Richard's language reflecting—or not reflecting—his emotional state, it can be fairly argued that most of the narrative looks back at a highly repressed man, and that the narrator uses language which mirrors this state. If a liberated narrator were to speak uninhibitedly of his past, then he would have to *describe* his previous state of repression, which would lead to a much wordier narrative. Evander has chosen to let his narrator *show* it through his language, which is entirely in keeping with the behaviorism he at this stage has not yet entirely discarded, and—more important—with his technique as a dramatist. In fact, the book's greatest merit could be said to lie precisely in the way the reader is directly confronted with a totally unvarnished account of Richard's frame of bloody-mindedness, his obstinacy, and his generally objectionable behavior.

It also does the book scant justice to posit a "happy end" and then to decry it as a sign of sentimentality. As Evander himself points out elsewhere, readers who think that Richard has thrown off all his difficulties at the end, have done so without reference to the personality presented to us in the text, and he adds that in none of his three latest novels has he done more than say "this is where something new starts."[10]

Something new started for Evander, too, after the completion of these three books. His sales had leaped, his two stage plays were being performed around the country. He was a household name. What was he to do next? He decided not to publish a book in 1976. Instead, he prepared a double bill for 1977.

The Snail and *The Case of Lillemor Holm*

On 21 January 1977, a novel called *Lungsnäckan* [The Snail][11] by the unknown writer Lillemor Holm was published by Bonniers and received a favorable notice in *Dagens Nyheter*. It appeared from the book's back cover that the author was twenty-five years old and that the novel was both autobiographical and her first published work. The reviewer spoke of the rather mechanical jargon which intermittently characterizes the narrative, but noted at the same time that "behind the everyday sleaziness and trendy slang, there lies literary talent concealed. . . . The author possesses black humor and intelligence, and swoops down on her own messy life as a bird of prey on its victim. There is neither romantic doom nor sentimentality here, but on the contrary a good dose of rough honesty."[12] Another reviewer wrote that, on beginning to read the book, he had felt sure that it was the work of a man, because of the remarkable similarity of its language to that of Per Gunnar Evander: "Here was the same calm, a trifle prolix narrative style, the same detachment, and the same indignation suddenly breaking through the slightly impersonal text."[13] He adds, however, that he gradually became convinced that it was, indeed, an authentic autobiography. The very fact that two reviewers can describe the book's style so differently is a small indication of its complex status. Our explanation is that a carefully planned narrative designed to appear as the work of an autodidact, is likely to contain contradictory elements, unless executed by a master of pastiche. At all events, the second critic was proved remarkably perceptive six months later, for what should Evander publish but a novel entitled *The Case of Lillemor Holm*, narrated by none other than the psychotherapist of the said Lillemor Holm, presenting his version of the story she had told in *The Snail*.

A great deal of evidence points to Evander as the author of both books, but let us save that discussion to the end, and start with a summary of *The Snail*, the autobiographical novel of Lillemor Holm.

The Snail.   Lillemor Holm, the daughter of a small-town school caretaker, is thoroughly repressed at home. Her father, who is himself bullied and condescended to by teachers, drinks and relieves his pent-up aggressions on his family. Her mother's chief preoccupation is keeping up appearances.

Lillemor fails her grades at school and gets a dreary job as cleaner at a local hospital. She is far from stupid, but her poor school record and her home upbringing have inculcated in her a sense of failure. One thing that makes her different is that she has second sight. It does her no good, however. When, for instance, she sees in a vision where her teacher's lost ring is to be found, she is merely accused of having stolen it in the first place. "I was practically looked on as a thief after that. Because no one believed that I had seen the ring inside my own head. That was just lies and rubbish from beginning to end, according to them. I was out on a limb with what I had seen and experienced and I hadn't a clue how to tell about it so that a single person would believe me" (37). In consequence, when she follows an inner voice which tells her not to go with friends to a dance, and their car is subsequently involved in a fatal collision, she dares not tell anybody: "It had to remain a secret, a terrible and somehow weird secret" (56). Later, she leaves home and joins a pot-smoking crowd, falls deeply in love with a student with whom she lives in Stockholm until she becomes pregnant and is forced by him to have an abortion.

After a first suicide attempt, she goes rapidly downhill, but manages to prevail upon an unwilling psychotherapist to take her as a patient. Although the therapist is reducing his commitments, since he feels the need for a year's sabbatical, he agrees to see her twice a week until the summer holidays, at which point he explains that she will have to go to someone else. At the end of the holidays she is overcome by misery and a sense of rejection (not improved by her importunate calls to her ex-boy friend, who merely swears at her), and she makes a second suicide attempt. She wakes up in hospital, and her therapist agrees to take her on again. The novel closes with the girl's account of how she lies in bed, curled into a ball, believing she can hear her dead father calling her name. He tells her not to be afraid and keeps repeating that he has something important to tell her. But he fades away, and she is left thinking about what he wanted to say: "Maybe it wasn't all that much, really. I guess maybe all he wanted to say was that he always liked me though he never said so when it really needed saying . . . maybe he just wanted to say that he loved me" (178–79).

Even this cursory outline establishes a number of links with Evander's earlier works: the social and emotional disadvantages of belonging to a menial group in society, the serious consequences of lack of parental encouragement and understanding, an interest in extrasensory perception, the pain of a terminated pregnancy, suicide as a reaction to loss of love, and a fetal position coupled with a reconciliatory vision. But let us move on to the book quite indisputably written by Evander, and return to *The Snail* when we have more facts at our command.

The Case of Lillemor Holm. On the surface, *Fallet Lillemor Holm* [The Case of Lillemor Holm] is the first-person account of the present predicament and recent past of a middle-aged psychotherapist nicknamed the Sole, who finds himself increasingly tired and unable to concentrate, and who, on medical advice, decides to take a year's leave. As this period of release draws near, he is approached by a young woman, the broad outline of whose life-story is already familiar to us from her book, *The Snail*. He unwillingly agrees to postpone his freedom for a few months, and promises to see her during the intervening period. Her attempted suicide, when she is left on her own after the initial period ends, leads to his continued involvement in her case. She shows signs of improvement and stabilization, and her final suicide comes as a shock and hits him as a professional failure. Shortly afterward, he himself takes thirty-nine nembutal tablets with half a bottle of whiskey and is found only just in time to be resuscitated.

In order to avoid disclosing too much information from the start, Evander—always fond of suspense and mystification—makes his narrator, the Sole, selective in what he reveals about his current situation, while he allows him to be open in his account of past events (within the constraints of a strictly chronological sequence). So although the reader has noted that the Sole is writing his retrospective account of the past three years in a borrowed country cottage where he is regularly visited on alternate Fridays by a friend from his student days, it is not until after the revelation of his client Lillemor's successful suicide—late in the book—that certain things become obvious. His friend is keeping an eye on him—after his own suicide bid—in his capacity as a doctor, and the whole book represents the Sole's attempt to understand what led to the double catastrophe.

The therapist as metaphor.   Read as a therapist's account of his dealings with a difficult "client" (the term preferred by him), the novel's long, seemingly verbatim exchanges between the two protagonists have an air of impressive authenticity. It can be argued, however, that this is not—except in a superficial sense—a book about a psychotherapist and his patient, but a book in which the author uses the work of a psychotherapist as a metaphor for his own craft of authorship and its associated problems, and it is from this perspective that it will be discussed here. It is only fair to add that reviewers of the book have all discussed it in terms of therapist and patient, and that it has been widely praised, sold, and discussed as an interesting book about psychotherapy.

It will by now be clear that in his writings Evander has repeatedly demonstrated the fateful effects of lack of parental love and encouragement, as well as the effect on the individual of institutionalized repression and exploitation. The notion of the writer as "psychotherapist" is therefore a fitting one. This is borne out by an interview in which the critic Matts Rying, suggesting that the psychological analysis of individuals found in Evander's books might function therapeutically for many readers, asked the author if he feels an affinity with clinical therapists? He replied that he does, in a way, see his writing as an element or stage in a psychotherapeutic process, which has been confirmed by letters he has received from readers who have identified with characters in his novels: "It feels grand to receive testimonies of that kind, then you know that you are engaged in something which is not altogether meaningless."[14]

When Evander has met with a lack of understanding of what he is trying to *say*, he has taken it much to heart. It is tempting, therefore, to see something of him in the Sole's declaration in *The Case of Lillemor Holm*, that he is "a person who has failed both as a human being and as a professional man" (25), and the same is true of his assurance that he, in his work as therapist, "has tried to give back to people what they . . . have lost in terms of self-confidence and independence" (26). There is an unmistakable correspondence between Evander's employment as a television producer with only limited time for writing, and the fact that the Sole seldom has been able to devote all his time to his therapeutic practice, but has had routine administrative tasks to deal with throughout his career. The Sole's temporary doubts about the value of his therapeutic method—"It seemed to me that psychotherapy was no more than a question of conforming, a substitute for real mutuality" (30), and that it might in a long term treatment "be positively harmful, since it could so clearly be utilized for manipulative ends" (31)—are transparently applicable to a writer going through a period of tired self-doubt. So the Sole's decision to take a sabbatical year, "in order to come to grips with my growing lack of faith in the therapeutic method" (31), can easily be seen as equivalent to Evander's own decision to take a break both from his writing and his job with Swedish Television during 1976, and to publish nothing during that year.

A woman in focus.   It has been remarked that Evander seldom wrote about women. We may remember, though, that he countered the observation by stressing what an immensely important role women play in the lives of his male characters. Nevertheless, these two books about Lillemor Holm represent a new departure in terms of their center of focus. It is arguable that this change of gender is more apparent than real, however, for on closer inspection we find that Lillemor shares her central experiences with her male precursors, and there are striking structural parallels between their respective existential situations. Lillemor curled up in bed, thinking that her father is calling out to her that he loves her, is a variant of Richard in *Earth Divine* curled up in bed recalling a family skating party on the ice.

The parallelisms between Lillemor and that other fragmented Evanderesque alter ego, brother Henning in *A Love Story*, is even more striking. Both youngsters have had a disturbed adolescence and have failed to fulfill parental and societal expectations, both are engaged in writing a book, both possess paranormal faculties, both are unhappily in love, and both ultimately commit suicide. An equally striking set of correspondences can be found between Lillemor and her therapist. Both attempt suicide and then act on professional advice to "write out" their problems. The Sole sometimes covertly examines his client Lillemor to see how she is reacting to his questions, just as his own doctor friend sometimes looks at him "in that typical doctor's way . . . as discreetly as you can possibly imagine" (239). When the Sole sits on an old wooden bench by the roadside waiting for his medical friend, it can be seen as a variant of the analyst's couch on which Lillemor spent so many hours. Both of them circle restlessly when under stress, like caged animals, and both declare that their respective therapists deserve a medal for putting up with them.

Suicide. It is obvious that the reader is intended to pick up the behavioral resemblances between Lillemor and her therapist. Both characters are also parties to the conflict between what we might call realism, on the one hand, and blind emotionalism—or fatalism, in the Sole's terminology—on the other. This is no simple contest, for the experienced, middle-aged therapist, who claims consistently to have tried to help his clients to see causal factors and connections in their lives, not only fails to help his client in this particular case, he actually succumbs to the suicidal impulse himself.

Since suicide plays a crucial role in both *A Love Story* and *The Case of Lillemor Holm* it would be easy to suppose that this fact is an illustration of what is sometimes regarded abroad as a particularly Swedish phenomenon.[15] In fact, the Swedish suicide rate is unremarkable in a comparative context, so let us instead make the bold assumption that the suicides of Henning and Lillemor are practical solutions to narrative problems.[16] Evander has no brother, and Lillemor Holm—for the sake of our argument—has never existed outside the printed page. If both these characters had been alive at the end of the novels in which they figure, their author and originator would have had two fictions to sustain—or rather, to disclaim. It is from both the formal and narrative points of view an elegant solution that brother Henning, who has never existed except as a projection of the author's personality, should die and leave his progenitor in his chosen solitary state. The same is true of Lillemor for even more pressing practical reasons. But Evander skillfully takes care not in any way to present her suicide as an inescapable consequence of her situation. He allows her to undertake certain precautionary measures which indicate that she was subconsciously hoping to be saved this time, too. Anything else would seem strange, in view of the fact that Evander is committed to a belief in the healing potential of psychotherapy and a rejection of social and psychological determinism.

Fatalism. In the context of this book, fatalism (*ödestro*) is illustrated by Lillemor's belief that she is a born failure, and that she cannot materially change the course of her life. A part of her is well enough to want to grow into a strong and independent being, but the passivity and destructiveness which, according to the book's logic, were engendered by her upbringing, are not easily overcome. It is in line with her general inability to assert herself as a well-integrated personality, that the only field in which she excells is clairvoyance, a talent which in our present state of knowledge ranks as inexplicable, socially unharnessed, and generally suspect.

It is noteworthy that thwarted love is a major factor contributing to Lillemor's unhappiness. For the rational response to thwarted adult love would be to transfer one's affections elsewhere—we must suppose—but Lillemor is of the opinion that one can only fall in love once in one's life, and she persists in loving the brutal Stephen despite his unequivocal rejection of her (just as in *A Love Story*, Henning's suicide note quite simply says, "I want to be with Anna," despite the fact that she had chosen to remain with her husband). The irrationality of these attitudes is highlighted by the narrator in each case finding the loved person objectively speaking unattractive.

The Sole himself is only too aware of the danger of irrational human passions. He has an abiding memory of the violent hatred shown him by his wife, just before their short-lived marriage broke down. Her uncontrolled passion was made all the more inexplicable by the gentle love which transformed her a few moments later when she embraced their small son. This same son, when adult, presents his father with food for thought when he gets involved in a fight at

Stockholm airport, and in the face of parental remonstrances proclaims that "sometimes a good smack in the face is better than a load of guff and cackle"(190).The Sole is not impressed by the argument, despite the fact that he tells his client Lillemor that it is essential to learn to be "straightforward in one's emotional responses" (250). These are intricate problems and Evander offers no easy solutions. That irrationality should not be countered by force, however, is clear from a painful memory of how the therapist once as a young teacher used force on a phobic pupil who had refused to pass under a high-voltage cable on a school outing, when the alternative was a detour of several kilometers. Looking back on the episode, twenty years later, he writes: "I don't want to believe that it [my action] was typical of me and my way of solving conflicts, I don't want to believe that I had so little sense of the need to treat people with care, particularly people of deviant behavior and reactions. I don't really want to believe that it ever happened" (25).

The radical critique. In that reading of the novel which sees the therapist as a metaphor for the author, the Sole's son represents the young generation of radicals who demand direct political commitment in literature. He says of his father's treatment of his clients, "you render them harmless, pa, you disarm those who try to revolt" (191). His father replies to this, that on the contrary it is before they have been helped by therapy that insecure people submit themselves meekly to authority, whereas treatment is designed to give them self-confidence and the ability to influence society and their own lives. If we transpose this to the field of literature, it suggests the hope that his books can speak to individuals and help them to see and hear and think independently (as opposed to "ideologically correctly").

The final chord. *The Snail* and *The Case of Lillemor Holm* are powerfully linked by a closing theme which seems to indicate that they were designed as a unity. Lillemor cannot bear to believe that her father did not love her, despite his behavior. Her recurrent vision is of him calling her name, and she then supplies the unspoken message which she so clearly wants to hear. This is the chord on which *The Snail* ends. *The Case of Lillemor Holm* closes with the Sole dialing his son's phone number twice, and then forgetting what he had meant to say.

But what had I got to say to Thomas? What was it that was so important that I actually took the trouble to borrow the telephone a second time? What was it that was so important that I immediately repressed it?

Did I want to reproach him for something? Did I want to apologize to him for something? I'll be damned if I can remember.

Or did I simply want to call him up and say that I liked him? Maybe I wanted to call up my own son and say that I loved him? (311–12)

Shortly afterward, the Sole recalls the last time he saw Lillemor alive. She had come to deliver the manuscript of her novel, and stayed only a moment before disappearing round the corner again. The Sole notes: "I did not get round to *saying anything more.* I just stood there following her with my eyes . . . neither the dogs nor I were ever to see her again" (313). [My italics.]

The parallels and correspondences both within *The Case of Lillemor Holm* and between the two books are meticulously worked out. We have in front of us an intricate literary artifact. Yet the cumulative suggestive power of the two books is so strong that we find ourselves forgetting Lillemor's fictive status and asking ourselves: "Could her suicide have been averted if the Sole *had* said something? Might she be alive if only. . . ?"

Who was Lillemor Holm? There was not a newspaper or magazine in Sweden in the autumn of 1977 which did not have an article about *The Case of Lillemor Holm* and a photograph of its author. Quite apart from the intrinsic merits of the book, which were freely acknowledged, Evander was big game for journalists who wanted an inside story and an explanation of how he had come to write a novel of three hundred and thirteen pages about the author of a book published six months earlier, an author of whom no one had ever heard before, and who now appeared (judging by Evander's book) to have committed suicide.

The back cover of *The Snail* states that "This is the first time the name Lillemor Holm appears on a book cover. The author introduces herself best in her book: born in 1951, her father a school caretaker, brought up in quiet, lower-middle-class surroundings in a small community. . . ."[18] At the time, this odd formulation about it being the first time the author's name was on a book cover passed unnoticed, but once Evander had sprung his bombshell with *The Case of Lillemor Holm,* the cryptic wording took on another significance. The publisher (of both books) would say nothing except that he had never met Lillemor Holm and that he could make no statement on her behalf. Evander himself claimed that he had known the girl and that "we agreed that I could use her 'case' in a book—which would not harm her, since she had already written about herself in her book *The Snail,*" and he went on to say that she was already dead when her book appeared.[19] Bonniers had evidently not got the situation quite so neatly sorted out in the spring of 1977, however, since the author of an article on literary debutants of 1977 wrote that unlike the other novices, who all had their photographs included, Lillemor Holm could provide no photograph and had sent a message through her publisher that she had no wish to meet journalists: "not at present, anyway."[20]

A leading critic wrote:

If we assume that Per Gunnar Evander, who is a well-known—indeed a famous—author, can scarcely be a pseudonym for Lillemor Holm, then the reverse must reasonably be the case. There are, of course, further alternatives. Per Gunnar Evander can, for instance, have had access to a manuscript by the person who is called, or calls herself, Lillemor Holm, which he then worked over in various ways.

No one need begrudge the author his success in writing two novels with, in part, the same material, but all the same, the mystification can strike one as something of a speculation in the market value of riddles.[21]

The present author ought to admit to an initial conviction, on reading *The Snail,* that Evander was its author. His subsequent assurances, in conversation, that he had merely handled the girl's manuscript and that this explained the stylistic and linguistic *Evander-isms* were temporarily persuasive. But study of both books and the weighing of inner and outer criteria establish beyond reasonable doubt that both books were designed and executed by the same author.

Evander says that he finds it humiliating and hurtful that critics have spent so much time discussing the provenance of *The Snail* and its relationship to *The Case of Lillemor Holm,* rather than concentrating on what he has tried to communicate. On a serious level, though, it is quite impossible to discuss two related texts without noting the signals (stylistic, thematic, and structural) which they emit. To do so would be to treat Evander's work with less attention than it deserves.

Evander's main concern with these two works was, clearly, the exploration of existential insecurity, and the idea of writing two interlocking works, each mirroring a client and her therapist—but from opposite points of view—was an original one, posing intricate narrative problems, very different from writing a book and its sequel. What was required was an initial text which would lend itself to scrutiny and penetration in the following text. The first book had at one and the same time to be credible as the work of a young, unliterary person, yet not so badly written as to be unreadable. It also had to be organized so as to bring out the major points which were subsequently to be elaborated in the second, weightier book. Certainly, *The Snail* is marked by literary devices which would be highly unlikely in the work of a genuine beginner, and it has a self-assured informality of a type credible in a sophisticated New York–bred adolescent like Holden Caulfield but less so in a young Swede with no literary background. The liberal sprinkling of expletives in such a carefully organized text produces a slightly artificial air. One journalist observed that the book "is written in adolescent male language. *The Snail* speaks with a language which I, at all events, thought was the prerogative of adolescent boys. A raw, direct language."[22] As though to counter this particular objection, Evander lets the therapist in *The Case of Lillemor Holm* remark that Lillemor's "overriding ambition to approximate to her own colloquial speech sometimes becomes mechanical, so that an almost masculine jargon takes over." (298) It is not hard to suppose that this remark was inserted into the proofs of his second book, after the author had noted critics' reactions to *The Snail.*

A harsh view of Evander's denial of the authorship of *The Snail* is that it can "be seen as a contribution to a public spectacle arranged by an author who, in all of his books, has played with changes of identity and 'borrowed names.' One can wonder about the motives behind the game, but it seems reasonable to suppose that when in *Lungsnäckan [The Snail]* Evander for the first time used a woman for his mouthpiece, it was to avoid the ever-increasing expectations of his critics and readers—and also to avoid all pseudo-debates about the ability of male writers to depict the female mind."[23]

Judas Iscariot's Clenched Fists

Evander's thirteenth novel—*Judas Iskariots knutna händer* [Judas Iscariot's Clenched Fists, 1978]—proved a radical departure from the contemporary Swedish environment of his previous fiction. He moved into the field of religious myth and legend which his compatriot Pär Lagerkvist had so memorably explored. Lagerkvist was awarded the Nobel Prize for literature in 1951 for his novel *Barabbas,* which has the crucifixion as its central dramatic event. Evander's novel describes the week culminating in the crucifixion as seen and experienced by Judas Iscariot. But where Lagerkvist shows us human beings faced with the divine—either as something or someone they recognize as representing a transcendental reality or as a persistent longing within themselves for transcendence—the concerns of Evander's novel are entirely of this world. He has written an apologia for Judas, who within his limitations appears decent and honest enough; a young man obsessed with political liberation, who cannot understand that Jesus's kingdom is not of this world. When Jesus at the last supper says that one of his disciples will betray him, and then, handing the morsel to Judas, "What you are going to do, do quickly,"[24] Judas thinks it is part of Jesus's grand strategy to allow himself to be arrested, in order to carry out a subsequent political coup.

Due to the limitations of his understanding, this Judas becomes an innocent scapegoat—which leads straight into the theological and moral complications of predestination as they pertain to Christ's sacrificial death, with Judas as the instrument of betrayal. We have Judas, the scapegoat, betraying the most innocent scapegoat of all time, Jesus Christ, who was sacrificed because the Pharisees reasoned that it was better that one man die for the people, and of whom Isaiah prophesied that he would be "led like a lamb to the slaughter."[25] But Evander's narrative is neither discursive nor religiously problem-orientated, and any working out of the consequences and ramifications of the situation he presents is left to the reader. The problems he has drawn attention to in interviews in which he discusses the book, are society's need for scapegoats—for example, Lieutenant Calley and the My Lai massacre and the continuing search for Nazi war criminals,[26] and seeing the disciples as constituting "a guerilla group with clear political aims."[27] In the latter connection he explains that "one of the aims of my novel is to de-mystify the group around Jesus and not make it foreign to guerilla groups of our day."[28] Initially, he says, he had intended to include "the Christian message in the novel, but I could not manage it. Partly, I felt I was too ignorant, and partly, it takes a long time to penetrate the mysteries of grace. Partly, too, I could not combine it with the ambition . . . to make the group more true to everyday life."[29]

Evander did a lot of homework on the figure of Judas: "At one time I thought of stating my sources, but that would have looked too pretentious,"[30] he told an interviewer. He visited Jerusalem, examining its surroundings and topography, and he read a number of "more or less inferior novels about Judas from Tor Hedberg to Eric Linklater."[31] It is interesting to note that within months of the appearance of his book on Judas, the Italian Giuseppe Berto (shortly before his death in December 1978) published the novel *La Gloria* (The Glory), which also rehabilitates Judas and sees him as an instrument of a historical necessity.[32] Then, early in 1979 came the Swedish novelist Göran Tunström's *Ökenbrevet* (Letter from the Desert) about Jesus during the years between his childhood and his ministry. And in March 1979 the Stockholm Opera performed a new opera, *Josef,* by Björn Wilho Hallberg (libretto by Karin Boldemann), in which the innocent young Mary, victim of a brutal rape, cannot face this reality and invents the story of the immaculate conception instead. Joseph, her betrothed, does not believe her, but his generous love impels him to stand by her all the same.[33] The two latter works, like Evander's, de-mystify and secularize biblical history, but they do it with a sense of the immanence (as opposed to the transcendence) of love; they deal with an eternal and life-giving principle. What is a little disappointing about Evander's book is its apparent lack of a broader philosophy of life; there is only the personal and indecisive drama of this one man, while the reader hopes for a secular version of a universal theme such as perdition or redemption. On the other hand, it is always interesting to hear the age-old story told anew, and the following outline will indicate some of the incidents and elements of Evander's version.

Outline of the novel.   The disciples and their Master are on their way to Jerusalem a week before the festival of the Passover. Judas, in his early twenties, is one of the youngest of the company. Jesus has long since been pronounced a blasphemer and troublemaker by the council and entering Jerusalem is bound to bring him into conflict with the authorities. Judas and his fellows believe that Jesus is the Messiah who has come to release his people from bondage, and Judas expects in an undefined way that this will result in speedy and triumphant political action.

Jesus restores the sight of a blind beggar, but Judas subsequently gets the impression that the man is still blind. Judas pays a call on friends, who are keen to hear details of the raising of Lazarus from the dead, but Judas was not an eyewitness of the event and stresses that such occurrences are superficial compared to the Master's mission to rid Jerusalem of unbelievers. As he urgently strives to convey his thoughts to them, he notices that he has clenched and raised his fists, "and when Judas notices both Jacob and his wife staring at him in surprise, he feels a little ashamed and calms down immediately and resumes his seat" (67). Subsequently, he considers it an unworthy mode of transport when Jesus chooses to enter Jerusalem riding on an ass, and his feelings are ambivalently torn between the enthusiastic hosannahs of the crowd and anger at the humiliation when the ass shies and Jesus slides to the ground. He visits his father, is present when Jesus drives the moneychangers out of the Temple, and gets into conversation with a woman, whom he unsuccessfully tries to convince of Jesus's messianic mission. As we have previously indicated, Jesus says at the meal the disciples eat together that one of them will betray him, and Judas interprets this remark as a commission representing a necessary link in an apocalyptic chain of events. After Jesus's arrest the other disciples scatter, and Judas finds himself in a narrow alley witnessing three men being led out to crucifixion. On recognizing Jesus in the mutilated figure of the foremost cross-bearer, he feels paralyzed and incapable of thought or feeling. In the same way, when he stands looking at his crucified Master, whom he had venerated as People's Liberator and King, it is as though the sight cannot register properly. Subsequently he starts to weep, beating his clenched fists (those iconographic references to a liberation movement) against a stone wall, crying: "Why did you fail me, Rabbi? Why did you do it? Why did you fail us all?" (194). The novel ends with Judas setting off toward

Jericho, feeling that if he can continue to walk and tire himself out, "he will soon shake off his restless anxiety, he is somehow sure of that. . . . It is true that it has been an exhausting day, but he still has plenty of strength left. . . . And he is still very young" (198). This indirect inner monologue on Judas's part strikes a note very obviously and deliberately at variance with biblical tradition.

Evander's Judas Iscariot. Evander has seized on the possibility that the name Iscariot could be derived from "sicarius," meaning dagger-man or assassin and links Judas with Simon the Zealot.[34] The latter takes Judas with him to see a famous prophet, one John the Baptist, leader of "something which might be the beginnings of a resistance movement" (32), we are told, and it is now that the two young men meet Jesus of Nazareth and become his followers. In addition, the possibility that Iscariot means "man of Kerioth"[35] (in South Palestine) has been used to good effect by Evander. Since the majority of the disciples were Galileans from the north of Palestine, and Judas on the Kerioth hypothesis was the only Judaean among them, it was natural for Jesus to choose him as messenger or "betrayer," since he knew his way about Jerusalem far better than the others.

How closely Jesus's spectacular ministry of healing and miracles became bound up in the popular imagination with the assumption of earthly power is emphasized by Ethelbert Stauffer in his study *Jesus and his Story,* which Evander acknowledges as one of his sources.[36] Stauffer points out that during Jesus's lifetime the political despair and expectations of Palestinian Jews had grown almost beyond bounds, and that the Passover was traditionally associated with the notion of the Messiah's advent and the establishment of the Kingdom. When Jesus performed his miracle of the feeding of the five thousand by the shores of Lake Gennesareth on the occasion of an earlier Passover, the people cried out: "This is indeed the prophet who is to come into the world!" and they wished to "come and take him by force and make him king."[37] When the chief priest and the Pharisees heard of the raising of Lazarus—a few months before the final Passover—they agonized: "What are we to do? For this man performs many signs. If we let him go on thus, everyone will believe in him, and the Romans will come and destroy both our holy place and our nation."[38] Yet a significant fact about Evander's novel is that while he most realistically stresses Judas's political aspirations, he chooses to let him show indifference to Christ's miracles—despite the fact that, as Stauffer points out, these two factors were so closely linked in the consciousness of Jesus's contemporaries. Indeed, the novel tells us explicitly that Simon and Matthew share Judas's attitude: "they regard the miracles as totally subordinate to the message, above all to what is now expected of the Master by practically all his supporters—namely, the restoration of the Kingdom of David" (137).

We know that Jesus sent out his twelve chosen disciples with the injunction: "Heal the sick, raise the dead, cleanse lepers, cast out demons."[39] But the novel renders this commission in the rather abstract form of "he chose twelve of them, who at the same time were given the task of spreading the teaching which many already regarded as the Master's own, and which at heart involved something entirely new" (31). Furthermore, Judas himself "was not one of the witnesses to the miracles, like most of the others he had only heard of these things at second hand" (66). In fact, as the anticipated hour of revolution approaches, he thinks to himself, "Miracles and boundless love of your neighbor may also be important elements in the Master's teaching, but none of that must be allowed to obtrude itself at this point in time" (58). A significant indication of how determined Judas is to reject the miracles is provided by his relationship to his father Simon Iscariot. The Bible merely mentions him as a name, but in the novel he is old, blind, and poor, and who could be more in need of a miraculous cure? Yet, Judas showed no interest in the possibility that Jesus might restore his father's sight.

Evander prefaces his novel with a motto by Kafka: "The believer experiences no miracles. You see no stars by daylight" (5). Must this not mean that people tend to regard what they believe in as natural and self-evident, hence something which, by definition, excludes the miraculous? If the stars of the motto, metaphorically speaking, represent the miraculous, then daylight represents the common-sense rationality which is incapable of perceiving the miraculous. In a sense we could argue that Judas's passionate conviction that Jesus—in some nebulous way—will inaugurate an era of glorious peace and Jewish liberty here and now, is precisely a demonstration of someone hoping for a political miracle. But to Judas, his political aspirations are real and rational; it is divine intervention in sickness and death which are mysterious, miraculous, and hence suspect.

Links with *The Case of Lillemor Holm.* Why does Evander exclude belief in the supernatural in his novel? An interpretation of *Judas Iscariot's Clenched Fists* might be that he has set up a confrontation between an ordinary mortal who represents typical secular twentieth-century aspirations—and the ultimate in "irrationality" or the supernatural, namely, Jesus, son of God. It seems, at all events, not unlikely that Judas is used to explore further the conflict between rationality and the irrational which is presented in *The Case of Lillemor Holm.* Judas feels marked uneasiness when faced with the supernatural, and in the same way, the psychotherapist in *The Case of Lillemor Holm* is guarded and skeptical in his response to his client's paranormal gifts—because he cannot explain them—and prefers to concentrate on the hard facts of her background and upbringing. His goal in life is to help people to an awareness of cause and effect and to provide a rational explanation of how these problems have arisen. He does not, however, succeed in saving Lillemor, who is a young woman driven by irrational impulses, and he very nearly goes under himself. It would seem that his therapeutic model leaves something out of account.

At this point a psychological hypothesis presents itself. Both the psychotherapist in his professional role, and Judas in his very different one, are basically insecure men seeking relief through certainties. "The truth shall make you free" is a biblical quotation which Evander says he often has in mind when writing his novels.[40] But the truth cannot be accounted for by exclusively rational, political, or social causative formulas. The fact that it is of such urgent importance for Judas to make an acquaintence, Rachel, understand what it is he believes in is indicative of his insecurity. He clenches his fists and speaks of Jesus's messianic mission, but she is entirely resistant to both the political and the supernatural aspects of Jesus's ministry. Judas finds it impossible to maintain his equilibrium in the face of her skepticism and flees from her, not wishing to see her again until after Jesus's imminent political triumph, or "when reality has come into line with his own expectations" (147). In the event, Jesus is shamefully humiliated and

crucified, and Rachel is the last person in the world Judas wishes to
see—for in meeting her he would have to confront his own failure to
integrate the inexplicable dimensions of Jesus into his world picture.

Judas's reaction to the crucifixion. The parallels between *The
Case of Lillemor Holm* and *Judas Iscariot's Clenched Fists* are worth
stressing. At the center of each novel is a man who must come to terms
with failure. The whole of the former novel is an attempt on the part
of the psychotherapist to analyze what has gone wrong in his life and
practice. The latter novel shows us how and why things went wrong
for Judas, and ends just as realization of the enormity of his mistake
begins to penetrate.

When Judas recognizes Jesus in the tortured figure stumbling under
the weight of his cross, he feels "as though he had been deprived of
the ability to think another straightforward thought for the rest of his
life" (184). His eyes register Jesus hanging on the cross, but the
message evokes no emotional response. All he feels is emptiness. Judas
is in a state of shock. As it gradually wears off, its place is taken by
confusion and anxiety. Tears well up and, weepingly, he reproaches
Jesus for failing him. He is like a child who is hurt and angry because
his parent has forced him to see something he did not want to see. It
is difficult, as the novel closes, not to feel that all Judas's energies are
devoted to containing his emotions and fighting off the realization of
what his actions have led to. It is a behavioral pattern familiar to us
from *The Physics Master's Sorrowful Eyes* and from *Earth Divine*.
Yet Evander's view of Judas's future, given in a newspaper interview,
is that "His despair is in itself enough. . . . Out of the remorse, anxiety
and torment a spiritually strong man may develop. . . . It is possible
that he will become an apostle in the true meaning of the word.
Personally, I feel that the passion drama becomes more interesting if
Judas is like one of us."[41]

It all depends on the degree of guilt and remorse we imagine that
Judas could live with, for in the novel he does not commit suicide. But
in fairness to Evander's open ending we must concede that Saul of
Tarsus made a famous convert, so why not Judas Iscariot? That would
indeed be the ultimate triumph of good over evil—the world's most
notorious traitor forgiven and redeemed.

Except that Evander's Judas is no traitor, strictly speaking, scarcely even a sinner. He is a confused young man who has made a big mistake.

Look Me in My Unblemished Eye

A big question mark hangs over Judas as he walks off into the night, his problems still unresolved. The close of Evander's next novel, *Se mig i mitt Friska öga* [Look Me in My Unblemished Eye, 1980], is by contrast confidently unambiguous. Let us start with a summary outline of it.

The book opens dramatically with fifty-year-old Adrian Lundgren coming in from the woodshed and cleaving his widowed mother's head with an ax. It is briefly indicated that Lundgren, divorced and living along with his mother, had been invalided out of his job at the local brickworks with severe damage to his back, and that constant pain and sleeplessness drove him to his inexplicable act of violence. The first person to enter the Lundgren home after the murder is the neighboring family's eight-year-old son Harold, who finds Lundgren sitting motionless on a chair while his mother lies outstretched on the kitchen floor. The little boy's pent up excitement bursts out of him later that afternoon when his parents are busy entertaining inquisitive locals with details of the affair and have little time for their son. "Ma! Ma! I'll never hack you with an ax!" he shouts, dancing wildly round her, "I'll never, never, never hack you with an ax!" (24).

The next time we meet Harold he is thirty-eight and has for some years made a living in Stockholm as a freelance writer of pornographic and—latterly—romantic magazine stories. A phone call from his home town in Gästrikland informs him that his widowed mother has died unexpectedly, but in response to the enquiry of the friends he is with, he says the call was just "something and nothing" (27) and goes to a football match with them as arranged. Halfway through the game, however, he slips away and gets on the first train bound for the north. As he sits on it, trying not to think of his mother, he remembers that a friend recently said to him, "Harold . . . in just over two years you'll be forty and your biggest fault is that you haven't a clue what a lot isn't going to happen to you before then" (33–34).

When he reaches his home town he finds that his sister is on sick-leave in a poor state of nerves. Both had found it hard to get on with their mother; his sister in particular has suffered from inability on her mother's part to understand that nervous trouble is an affliction that requires compassion and insight—particularly from parents. His sister's great prop is Martha, an extraordinarily kind and helpful teacher, who initially arouses ambivalent feelings in Harold. Before long a mutual liking develops between them, however, and when she makes it clear to Harold how much she cares for him, he decides to stay on in the town. Martha's seven-year-old son was killed on the motorway three years earlier, so she also has a bereavement to cope with, but her emotions—unlike those of Harold and his sister when faced with their mother's death—are unambiguous, and her profound grief is balanced by an equally strong sense of being in loving contact with the boy. Martha is the undoubted heroine of the novel and functions as life-giving friend, lover, mother, and daughter. She encourages Harold to believe in himself and his literary ambitions. He finds it increasingly impossible to write magazine stories and signs on for temporary work at a small local factory. We are given a picture of a rural area where one industry after another has been closed down and where even the branch line of the railway has met the same fate. Harold spends his days in a paint workshop and is badly affected by the fumes, which in conjunction with the indifference shown by the foreman and manager helps him to recall exactly what it was like to work at the brickworks twenty years earlier. Ever since then he has been storing up resentment against the working conditions he was subjected to and his father's disapproval when he threw up the job. It is clear that these emotions cannot be exorcised until he gets round to writing about his past instead of producing trash for publication.

Harold reestablishes contact with Adrian Lundgren, who has recently returned to the area after close on thirty years in hospital. He is able to do something for the old man and even brings himself to say "I do like you so much, old Uncle Lundgren, I want you to know that I sure do like you a lot!" (262). As the book draws to a close Harold and Martha persuade his sister to go into hospital for treatment, Martha feels able to leave the vicinity of her son's grave and move south to a new job near her mother, and Harold reaches the point where he can make the symbolic gesture of divesting himself—in the disused brickworks—of every garment except his underpants and setting off south, too, along the highway. He plans to buy a new set of clothes when he reaches the first town, and he steadfastly abstains from looking back in the direction from which he came.

Three major themes.   It is possible to discern three major themes in this novel and for simplicity's sake we can label them pornography or trash, murder, and bereavement. (For clarity's sake let us note that although all three were standard ingredients of Victorian trashy literature, murder and bereavement do not function as equivalents of pulp/pornography in this novel but are seriously meant.

Pornography.   Harold is presented as a man full of resentment at not having received any encouragement to pursue his literary bent as a young man. In a drunken monologue which signals the dramatist Evander at work, he rails against his fate:

Hell, I could have become a Jan Fridegård if I hadn't been forced to stay here and shrivel up because ma and pa wanted it. I could have become a Vilhelm Moberg! If only I could have started in time and they hadn't put their heels on my throat! If the folks who were the only people I cared about had just once said that I was any good. That I could achieve something! That I meant something! Hell, hell, hell . . . hell. . . . (137)

But because his parents only laughed at his ambitions he wasted eight years as a laborer and then after moving to Stockholm, eight years writing trash for magazines under pseudonyms. Now and again he has smuggled reminiscences from his working life and occasional social criticism into his stories, and he has liked to think that he has been keeping his hand in so as one day to write a "really honest account, one based on his own experiences, which will provide a measure of redress both for himself and for others who are oppressed either emotionally, financially or simply in moral ways" (108).

The notion of pornography or trash has implications both for Harold's livelihood and for his private life. On the one hand it covers the saleable commodity of which he is ashamed and from which he plans to escape by beginning to write about *real* life. Apart from the novel's symbolic ending which signals a new life ahead, it is clear that Harold actually does embark on his new way of writing, since he says to a workmate at the factory that he knows exactly how his books will start: "I've thought of opening with Adrian Lundgren bringing down a wood-ax on his mother's head" (281)—and this, as we know, is how *Look Me in My Unblemished Eye* opens. Evander's novel is, in effect, a counterpart to Harold's book. Exactly what metaphorical significance the term "trash" has for Evander himself is hard to speculate about at this stage. It is self-evident that pornography in the normal sense is absent from his books—with the possible exception of the boiler-house scene with the nymphet in *Dear Mr. Evander.* Conceivably, breaking with pornography could figuratively speaking be a question of achieving the freedom and self-confidence to be utterly resistant to the pressures of literary fashion; the writer as whore is an image with considerable currency in Sweden of the 1960s and 1970s, as Sven Delblanc demonstrated powerfully in his novel *Grottmannen* [The Troglodyte, 1977].

On the other hand pornography implies the exploitation and deformation of sexual relationships between human beings, and since our interpretation of Evander's text in this respect is conjectural, let us first rehearse the material.

Before their mother's funeral, Harold visits his sister and finds her very disturbed. He also meets Martha for the first time. They all drink a good deal, and when his sister gets desperate at the thought of being left alone, her visitors agree to lie down one on either side of her in her wide bed. Harold gets so hot on this summer night that he subsequently takes his clothes off. When he wakes up later he finds that his sister has moved to the sitting room sofa, leaving him and Martha, both naked, in her bed. The scenario is indisputably that of a pulp magazine story. It is redeemed by the fact that Harold lacks the confidence to make a bold pass at Martha, instead he gradually edges toward the center of the bed—believing her to be asleep—and lies there irresolutely until finally abandoning himself to sleep again. (Martha later admits to having been awake the whole time.) Immediately after this episode we are presented with a banal anecdotal reminiscence; in the aftermath of an authors' meeting at a hotel, Harold had arranged to spend the night with an unknown woman as drunk as himself, he entered a darkened room, undressed, and got into bed. His further exploits were interrupted by "the most enraged howl emitted by an elderly lady that had ever been heard at the hotel in question and in the surrounding neighborhood" (98). Either he had got the wrong room number or he had been taken for a ride. The nonplussed reader tries to determine the status of these scenes. Are they parodies of cheap magazine stories? And if so, ought not Harold to realize this? The following episode takes place in the local church, outside which he has arranged to meet Martha after she has finished rehearsing an end-of-term service with her pupils. He gets tired of waiting, enters the church instead, and says ominously that he has something important to tell her. Martha is alarmed and they go into the sacristy, where after some more simulated solemnity Harold says how much he likes her and how glad he is that she persuaded him to stay on. They embrace and end up by tumbling into a cupboard full of clerical vestments, where they have intercourse standing among the chasubles, all the time keeping a rather nervous weather eye on the unlocked door, to the faint accompaniment of the children's hymn singing. One subsequent evening, Harold and Martha make love out of doors, alarmingly close to neighboring houses, but he has to break off when "his organ rapidly shrinks to a snail and he is quite unable to continue their violent and serious game" (193). Instead, they turn to speaking of profoundly important things such as Martha's dead son.

Taking the above events as a whole, we can venture the opinion that Evander is not parodying pornographic situations but demonstrating that the distinguishing mark of a sexual relationship based on mutual trust and affection is not its outer framework—which can closely resemble that in a trashy magazine—but the state of mind of the protagonists. That the decisive factor is not the situation but the response of the individuals concerned and that the book shows us Harold subverting pornographic situations by the authenticity of his relationship to Martha. 216593

Murder. On the surface there is a striking resemblance between *The Story of Joseph* and *Look Me in My Unblemished Eye*. In both books a middle-aged worker, invalided out of his employment by intolerable conditions, kills the person closest to him in life. In fact, the in-depth parallel between the two books is that between the aging worker Joseph and the writer Harold. The figure of the matricide Adrian Lundgren is, in our view, a literary device designed to highlight the overriding emotional significance of the child-parent relationship for the little boy whose development we are to follow. We recall the deft plagiarizing of the manner of Old Icelandic sagas in the description of the fatal blow dealt to Lundgren's mother, "The action was executed with admirable precision and it is said that whoever saw the blow would have considered it successful" (12), and if we link this to the boy Harold's excitedly overwrought assurance that he will never kill his own mother, yet recall that as an adult he does so repeatedly in dreams, then we recognize the literary motif of *fate*. Harold is destined, not by the Norns—the old Norse fates—but by his own upbringing, to wage a long battle against parental oppression and his own repressed aggressions. He does not explicitly forgive his parents, but his determination to leave his old life behind him at the end of the novel seems to signify a move in this direction, and his association with Martha—who loves her own mother dearly, regarding her "more as a friend than a mother" (272)—is a hopeful sign.

Bereavement. The third major theme is bereavement, and it seems justifiable to mention that Evander's wife's seven-year-old son from her previous marriage died suddenly in August 1977. The ensuing grief has clearly helped to shape this novel.

The book opens with a man inflicting bereavement upon himself by killing his mother. It continues with another man receiving news of his own mother's death and traveling to her funeral. Here he meets a woman whose young son was killed three years earlier; he also has occasion to meditate over his parents' tombstone, to recall his late grandfather's grief at losing a thirteen-year-old daughter, and he once more comes into contact with the matricide Adrian Lundgren. The unspoken question throughout is how are we to live with the dead. It is Martha who shows us how it can be done:

> Do you often come here to the grave, he then asked.
> Not as often as I used to, perhaps.
> But you think of him pretty often, do you?
> Often is too weak a word really, because I actually think of him constantly, he's inside me the whole time, he's in every thought I have, in every emotion I feel, in every step I take, even if I just go to the window and wonder what the weather is going to be like he's with me, close, close to me. . . . It's my way of surviving, otherwise I might as well dig a hole next to him and curl up inside it. I've been close to it at times. (214)

When she places fresh flowers on her son's grave and rakes up twigs and leaves, she "moves swiftly and lightly like a very small girl, and it is as though there were joy and the profoundest trust in everything she undertakes" (255). Harold is aware of what a contrast this is to his own motionless stance at his parents' grave. Symptomatically, Adrian Lundgren's last request to him is that he should buy a candle at Adrian's expense and light it on Mrs. Lundgren's grave "and say hello to her from me, you can say it quite softly in case someone should be listening, just whisper and say hello from me" (290).

It is through love that all three themes—pornography, murder, and bereavement—find their resolution, one could even speak of their transcendence. The novel takes its title from a prefatory text which speaks of man's two eyes, one bad and sick and the other good and unblemished, and of mankind crying out down the centuries: "Stern fellow creature, merciful judge and executioner! Don't dwell upon what is bad and imperfect in me but recognize the good in me! Don't look me in my bad and sickly eye, look me in my unblemished one." (7). We realize that this was Harold's unspoken plea throughout his childhood and youth. And we divine that it is now the turn of his parents in their grave to direct the plea to him.

The verb "divine" is used advisedly. Evander has a tendency in this novel to juxtapose scenes and to introduce anecdotes which have little demonstrable bearing on its main stream. This can sometimes lead us to conclude that, while we may be overinterpreting his text, he on the other hand may not always be conscious of the logic of his own material. A different but related point is raised by a reviewer who notes that "Peripheral items and anecdotes are accorded notably generous space. While the central action is rather too often recounted in abstract, semiofficialese summaries."[42] To use a famous distinction, Evander alternates between telling us and showing us. His plays, to which the next chapter is devoted, for obvious reasons of genre lack this duality. For in them telling and showing become one, as episode, action, and speech combine. So they do in his most recent novel *Angslans boningar* [Fear's Dwelling Place, 1980], which lies— beckoning invitingly—strictly speaking beyond the scope of this study, but clearly requiring a brief presentation.

Fear's Dwelling Place

We recall that in *The Upstarts*, the writer Hadar Forsberg enters
into his own fiction and landscape, with a creative—as opposed to
escapist—intent, and that Evander in this way dialectically countered
Sven Lindqvist's *Myth of Wu Tao-Tzu* (cf. chapter 3). Ten years
later, *Fear's Dwelling Place* can be seen as counterpointing a new
book by Lindqvist, *Gräv där du står* [Dig where you are][43], a
handbook in do-it-yourself research into your place of work, which
aims to show ordinary workers and employees how to utilize archive
material, letters, diaries, the recollections and experiences of ordinary
people, etc., with a view to understanding how the economic system
works, as a prerequisite to changing it. Throughout the previous
decade, Evander had been made to feel obscurely guilty about using
his own experiences as material for his books. Now the seal of approval
had been affixed to personal material used for political ends. What,
we may ask, had for so long rendered this same material suspect in
literature? Answer (presumably): the writer's idiosyncratic, creative
and subjective structuring of his material.

Let us try to indicate how the dialectic orthodoxy/individualism
functions in the novel.[44] The action consists largely of the narrator
going to the aid of an old friend, Henry, an ex-building worker
suffering from a fatal liver disease, who lives in the country and whose
water supply pipe has sprung a leak. It is winter and the ground is
solidly frozen. Together the two men, but mostly the narrator, set out
to uncover by means of digging, the entire length of the pipe—some
two hundred and sixty yards long—until they find the leak. Amaz-
ingly, the whole laborious enterprise makes compelling reading. Nor
can onlookers within the fiction resist coming to watch. Gradually, the
attentive reader realizes that this digging must surely be a metaphor
for the writer at work. The narrator digs to find the leak—which
(being translated) is an unseen threat, an insidious fear, in short—
Henry's *angst*. Opinionated bystanders advise him to use an instrument
which would locate the leak acoustically, *above the ground*, in under
two hours, after which a mechanical earth shifter would do the rest.
Henry, when informed, firmly rejects the advice and asks the narrator
if he knows why he never became a first-class runner? It was because

he always had to be so damned tactical. "You always kept a weather-
eye on the fellows you were competing against, you hardly ever ran
your own race and as a result you never realized your potential" (90),
and he clinches the argument by exclaiming, "To hell with what
Rudén [their most persistent critic] says. We're going to keep digging
until we find the leak!" (90)

There are, figuratively speaking, other "leaks" besides Henry's. We
hear of the narrator's psychiatrist aunt and her unavailing struggle to
help a "disappearing" patient,[45] we hear of Henry's wife's clandestine
love affair (which Henry obscurely senses), we hear of the narrator's
own broken engagement to a girl who twice attempted to shoot him,
and last but not least, we hear of his brother Henning. We also hear
the narrator's confession that he had long wanted to write about his
aunt, but his courage had previously failed him, because he saw
himself "floundering in one of the many private man-holes which we
have incessantly been warned about" (70). Now he has finally realized
how false these "opportunistic" (70) warnings were.

This bald summation of the book can convey no idea of the
freshness of the text and its dialogues, nor the total conviction
conveyed by the description of the toil in the trench. At his best—
which this book represents—Evander makes reality and symbol
overlap totally. The more interested the reader is in semiotics, the
more significances he discovers. The three deaths in the book underline
the existentialist proposition that only *I* can die my own death. Death
is at the same time the most universal and most private of events. And
before dying, I need to understand what my life has been about. So I
have to dig. The trench both reveals my roots and prefigures my grave.
Neither the individual nor the writer can buy his way out with
mechanical aids.

Chapter Five

The Dramatist

Evander's ability to convey the thoughts and emotions of inarticulate people, coupled with the elements of absurdism in his early plays, might suggest Harold Pinter as a formative influence at the time of his debut as a radio dramatist in 1966. But he explains that "at the time I didn't know who Pinter was."[1] When he subsequently became familiar with *The Caretaker* and *The Birthday Party*, he admired them but had already found his own idiom. The absurdism in his radio plays derives directly from the stories in his own *Close Relations*, which had Kafka as its main stylistic inspiration.

When pressed to acknowledge an admired master,[2] Evander chooses Strindberg, particularly his late works, the "chamber plays." These short works, their collective designation indicating a loose parallel to the scale of orchestral chamber music, were written for a small intimate theater with a small cast. They are characterized by a concentration of theme and a mingling of the realistic and the fantastic—precisely the features which distinguish Evander's radio plays. He also mentions the importance to him of Strindberg's handling of the family situation—prime examples being *The Father* in terms of the naturalistic plays and *The Ghost Sonata* and *The Pelican* among the chamber plays. O'Neill's wrestling with family relationships in *Long day's journey into night* as well as his lighthearted treatment of them in *Ah, Wilderness!*, have also inspired him.

Radio plays 1966–1973

Radio theater is a popular art form in Sweden—an investigation in 1965 showed that a radio play (including repeats) reached an audience of between 300,000 and 500,000.[3] Not only have a great many Swedish novelists at some time or other written radio plays during the past quarter century—as the annual volume of selected plays published by the Swedish Radio Corporation testifies—but it was through the radio that Swedish audiences first became acquainted with the big names in international theater such as Pinter, Adamov, Beckett, and Albee.

The years 1967–1969 saw the emergence of political theater in Sweden, notably the work of a group centered around Bengt Bratt and Kent Andersson at the City Theater of Gothenburg and another at the Royal Dramatic Theater in Stockholm. The Swedish radio play, however, was less affected by the ideological climate of the time and functioned as a freer outlet for imagination. In the words of the foreword to the annual volume of radio plays for 1970, the plays "exemplify the scope radio drama offers to a variety of individualities. We are conscious of given boundaries, but also sense a freedom—in respect of narrative, in the description of environment and period, as well as in lyrical terms. . . ."[4] Certainly Evander's plays convey his existential concerns without the documentary formalism and the elaborate distancing effects used in many of his novels from the same period.

The fact that Stig Dagerman, whom Evander much admired, was the leading young dramatist of his generation until his early death in 1954, and that his plays—like Strindberg's expressionist dramas—relied on a suggestive, symbolistic presentation of human dilemmas rather than on realism and plot, cannot have been without significance for Evander. The short lyrical plays, with an absurdist streak, of Werner Aspenström (b. 1918), Dagerman's contemporary and literary associate, also form part of this background. The question arises, having indicated this link back to exponents of the stark pessimism of the 1940s generation, whether the absurdistic resolutions to many of Evander's plays—and of the short stories in *Close Relations* from which some of them are derived—are "philosophical" in the sense that they represent a view of life which sees human existence as absurd and meaningless. Or whether the unrealistic endings are to be taken as representing the inner emotional states of the central protagonists in situations which are not a priori but simply de facto.

Since there is no evidence that Evander regards human existence as intrinsically absurd, the first alternative can be discarded, and we are left with plays expressing varying degrees of *individual* fear, longing, and hope.

Debut in 1966.   Already as a schoolboy Evander had dreamed of becoming a theatrical producer, but when he told the job guidance counselor about it, he was firmly advised to put it out of his mind and become a teacher instead. It would have required far greater self-confidence than he possessed at the time to persist with his seemingly unrealistic hopes. They revived briefly when he came to Uppsala as a student, but the self-assured superiority of the student theater leaders there led him to withdraw, hurt. All the while, however, he listened to radio plays, and it was while teaching at a folk high school early in 1966 that he expressed his forceful contempt for a play he had just heard, thereby irritating a colleague who challenged him to write a better one himself. He picked up the gauntlet and wrote his first radio play, *Det är söndagseftermiddag, min bror springer på åkern* [It's Sunday afternoon and my brother's running across the field], in two evenings flat and sent it in to the Swedish Radio Corporation.[5] Carl Olof Lång, head of the drama section, recalls the play being received, recorded, and broadcast all within a week, directed by Lång himself and with an exceptionally fine cast.[6]

A married couple have their grown-up son, Max, home for a Sunday visit. The father is irritable, the mother conciliatory and weak, the son an evident liar. It appears that Max has told his mother that he has been offered a dream job, but when challenged by his father he answers evasively that he is not sure that he will be taking the job.

FATHER: You're stuck as a clerk on a pittance in a one-horse town, and
            when you're offered a job in Stockholm with twice the salary
            and a two-roomed apartment thrown in, you say that maybe you
            won't take it. Does that sound sane?[7]

Both men reinforce one another's negative responses while the mother tries ineffectually to smoothe things over.

MOTHER: Max dear, why must you stand by the window the whole time?
            There's a nasty draught there. . . .

FATHER: It's easier for him to spin his yarns when he has his back to us.
MOTHER: Now don't be unkind, dad dear. You'll see that that job in Stockholm will sort itself out.
FATHER: (*Under his breath*) He can make you believe anything![8]

It is symptomatic that when his father puts Max down by comparing him unfavorably to two local brothers who have graduated successfully, Max should stress the fact of them being a duo: "that makes two against one, so to speak."[9] We sense that Max is an only child whose situation has continuously been defined in terms of two against one; mother and father against Max, the outside world against Max. So our interest is aroused when we hear that a girl friend of his is coming to tea. From his father's sarcastic remarks it becomes clear that Max has a high turnover in girl friends. When pressed for details of the new girl, Barbara, he tells his parents that her father is a professor of medicine in the university town of Uppsala.

On arrival, Barbara embarrasses Max by revealing that he has spoken to her of marriage, but the news about the dream job in Stockholm, on the other hand, comes as a complete surprise to her.

BARBARA: . . . I don't exactly know if I could feel at home in a city.
FATHER: But don't your parents live in Uppsala?
BARBARA: In Uppsala? No, what makes you think so?
FATHER: But your father works there, doesn't he, Miss Berg?
BARBARA: My father died when I was three years old.
MOTHER: (*Sympathetically*) Oh dear!
BARBARA: He was a bricklayer here in this town.
FATHER: Really. Well, I must just have misheard. Isn't that so, Max?
BARBARA: (*To Max*) Have you said that my father is alive and that he lives in Uppsala?
MOTHER: It must be a misunderstanding.
FATHER: Quite so. It happens all too easily in conversation with our son.[10]

The biggest revelation of all comes when Barbara asks after the (nonexistent) brother Max has spoken so much about. When the young people are left alone together, the good-natured Barbara asks for an explanation. Instead of answering, Max beckons her across to the window and asks if she can see a figure in the field across the road in the rapidly failing light.

BARBARA: (*Eagerly*) Yes, now I can see it. There's someone running, leaning forward, just like a shadow.
MAX: You can see him, can't you?
BARBARA: Why sure, he seems to be in a hurry.
MAX: He *is* in a hurry, too.
BARBARA: How can you know that?
MAX: He's afraid, you see.
BARBARA: What of?
MAX: Of me. He hardly knows how to get home before dark. . . . Can you guess who it is?
BARBARA: Can't say that I can.
MAX: That's my brother.
BARBARA: What nonsense you're talking, Max! You haven't got a brother. . . .
MAX: It doesn't matter what you say and believe, he's my brother all the same. . . . It's just the way it is, it's nothing to get excited about. It's just the way it is. . . .[11]

We are left with the incontrovertible truth of personal existential states. The need for a brother to compete with and to frighten is the most real thing in Max's life.

After his success with this play, Evander wrote three more in quick succession, on the strength of which he was taken on as dramatist and producer by the Swedish Radio Corporation in the fall of 1966. *Hadar skulle säkert förstå* [Hadar would be sure to understand] presents a young man in extreme need. Fleeing from his enraged father, who is after him with a gun, he seeks shelter from—and is denied it by—a neighboring farmer. The situation recurs in essence in the novel *Dear Mr. Evander,* from the fugitive's perspective, and ten years later from the perspective of the pursuer in the television film *The Return* (1976). Here the perspective is that of onlookers afraid of getting caught up in the troubles of others. The farmer refuses to help on the ostensible grounds that he has not the time to involve himself because he cannot keep the eponymous Hadar waiting. His wife has stirrings of conscience once the young man has been sent packing and urges her husband to call the village and make enquiries.

FARMER: I haven't time. Hadar has been kept waiting long enough. I must go.
WIFE: He would be sure to understand if you were late. He's kind.
FARMER: Sure. But he has already had to wait too long. I'll do it tonight.[12]

The play's ironic title emphasizes that a deep-seated unwillingness to share other people's fear will seek any alibi, even the most irrational. By contrast, *Inte ska du gråta* [There, there, don't cry], shows us how human kindness can transform life. Two men are whiling away the time before a football match by drinking beer in a café. John has recurrent periods of depression, when life seems utterly meaningless, and his friend Edwin makes a variety of well-meaning suggestions— none of which are the slightest use. Then Edwin mentions his caretaker's daughter, who used to suffer from depression and not want to see anybody. When she sat in her room crying, her father would go in to her and gently put his large hands on her shoulders and say, "There, there, don't cry, Marie-Louise. Look at me. I'm not crying."[13] And it would work. "She tried to do away with herself several times, but each time her dad saved her. It was as simple as that. Just a few words at the right time. And a pair of hands on her shoulders, that's all that's needed sometimes."[14] John is still resistant to Edwin's remarks as they set off for the match. But the thought of the caretaker helping his daughter reverts to him at intervals as a meaningful gesture in what had seemed a meaningless world.

On Christmas Eve 1966, listeners were treated to a Christmas play with a difference, specially commissioned from Evander. The action of *Överraskningen* [The Surprise], as it was called, takes place on Christmas Eve, too. A middle-aged couple have invited the wife's unmarried sister to stay, for whom they have planned a nostalgic surprise in the shape of the caretaker coming in with their presents at 6:00 P.M., dressed as Father Christmas. They patronize the childless sister and proudly display the snapshots their son, training as a chef in England, has sent of his well-connected English fiancée. They exude self-satisfaction and bodily well-being after a first-class Christmas dinner. Then the doorbell rings and the wife goes to open it in the comfortable conviction that it must be the caretaker, come to crown a pleasant evening with their little surprise.

It turns out to be a far bigger surprise. It is their son, shabby and unshaven. He has no fiancée and has attended no course. Nothing in his letters was true. He is still as lonely and isolated as he was when he lived at home. His father is outraged: "He can't just turn up and spoil our Christmas. . . ."[15] It is the childless aunt who makes the son welcome and finds him something to eat in the kitchen. At this point the doorbell rings. "We'll let *them* open,"[16] says the aunt, leaving the listener to picture the caretaker dressed as Father Christmas and the embarrassed anger of the parents who were capable of make-believe Christmas bonhommie but incapable of welcoming a human being in need of love and understanding.

There is something Ibsenesque about the play's situational ironies and neat construction, as well as its unmasking of hypocrisy. What makes it Evanderesque is the figure of the lonely young man who tells tall stories, and his parents who regard their son as a family possession which either sheds lustre or disgrace on them. *I min ungdom speglade jag mig ofta* [In my young days I often looked at myself in the mirror, 1970] nicely varies the theme of egocentric inability to love. It reflects a fifty-five-year-old man's grotesque refusal to accept his own aging process and shows him projecting all his fear of senescence and death onto his wife, three years his junior, whom he finds repulsive, with sagging breasts, greasy grey hair, wrinkles, and a failing memory: "It's like living with my own mother."[17] When his wife is out, he summons his grown up children and in the name of family solidarity impresses on them that they must help to free their mother from her suffering (i.e., help to give her an overdose): "Don't you realize that she notices the same thing as you? That I am still in the full flush . . . well, as you said yourselves . . . that I still look youthful and strong. And don't you realize that she notices that other women have their eyes on me?"[18] The son suggests that his father might first try buying his wife some ladies' pornography, but is told that he ought to be ashamed to profane his mother. The children next urge divorce as a preferable alternative to murder, but father bellows angrily: "Murder! Who the hell has used that word? Why don't you listen! We're out to help ma! *Help!* Don't you understand standard Swedish!"[19] He recalls their young married days when they would both stand in front of the hall mirror and look at each other with delight. If he now catches sight of her in the mirror, it makes him shudder. Worst of all, he sometimes dreams that he is standing in front of a mirror and sees a bent and dirty old man. To underline his grievance, he shows the children photographs of how his wife *used* to look, and recalls getting to know her when he was a patient and she a young nurse with the smoothest skin and softest voice: "I remember that I had a hell of a fever and that I was about to burn up. . . . But she sat at the side of my bed and stroked my hair and forehead as though I was her own child."[20]

He married a young "mother," yet lacks the wisdom to accept an aging one. But the sharp satirical bite of the dialogue ends in lyricism as he relives his youth.

Smultrontrollet [The Wild Strawberry Troll, 1967] is an accomplished mixture of friendly family banter in a realistic and attractive Swedish summer setting on the one hand, and a suggestive, supernatural element on the other. A married couple and their teenage daughter Maria have just finished a cheerful lunch. The father has made a wooden cover to lay over a deep disused well on the hillside, where wild strawberries grow luxuriantly. When Maria was small, her parents used to keep her away from the well by saying that a troll lived in it. While her father now goes to fetch the lid, she calls "holloa" into the well, and is startled when the voice of a young man answers "hollo" out of its depths. To her eager questions of who he is and where and when he got into the well, he laughs and says he cannot remember, and when she eagerly promises to call for help, he forbids her to tell anyone of his presence. He recalls that he once knew a girl called Maria, with whom he walked in the woods and fed the swans. Maria asks "romantically, expectantly" if he was unhappy, but he answers evasively that there was something wrong with everything up there, and that he has accustomed himself to the cold and the dark of the well. Maria is childishly excited by her new friend, but a week later she returns moody and hurt, accusing him of having lied to her, for her father has cleaned out the well and pronounced it entirely empty. The young man assures her that it is possible to hide at the bottom of it and asks her to stretch her arm down so they can reach each other. Giggling uncertainly and a little scared, she complies, but cannot reach far enough. The final scene takes place in the cottage. Maria's father has just finished blocking up the well with boulders and his wife says that as soon as Maria heard about it she rushed out. "Perhaps she just wanted to admire my handiwork!"[21] laughs her unsuspecting father. The listener, on the other hand, feels a chill round the heart. Can Maria live without her dreams? And what about the young man? At what level of symbolism are we to take the play?

The young man in the well is invisible. So is Max's brother. And so are many of the characters who people Evander's radio plays. They are invisible either because they exist only in somebody's imagination or because they are humble and powerless in society. But they are indisputably *real.* To Miss Olson in the play *Medan dagen svalnar* [As day grows cool, 1968], a patient at a psychiatric clinic, the baby daughter for whom she is knitting a garment is absolutely real, although not to the brisk nurse who humors her. Sister Karin's benevolent authoritarianism masks emotional repression and prudishness. Miss Olson, on the other hand, can recall episodes of great happiness in an otherwise problematic existence. She and her friend Harry walked across the water together, holding hands. He laid his arm round her shoulders and squeezed them and she felt quite safe.

MISS OLSON: We didn't even notice we were walking across the water until we had nearly reached the middle of the lake. . . . I have never told this to anyone else, Sister Karin. You are the first person.

SISTER KARIN: *(With scarcely concealed irony)* I feel honored by that, Miss Olson. . . .

MISS OLSON: Harry. They shot him in the war after that. . . .

SISTER KARIN: Dear Miss Olson, what are you talking about? We haven't had a war for over a hundred and fifty years.[22]

The play alternates between the two women in flashback conversation on a bench by a lakeside and a sobbing Sister Karin telling a doctor that something terrible has happened. What it is, is not revealed until right at the end, when we hear Sister Karin telling her patient that it is time for dinner. Then suddenly, she sounds agitated:

SISTER KARIN: Where are you going. Don't go down to the water. We are already late. Do you hear me, Miss Olson! Come back I say! . . . Wait. Don't go out! *(Shrilly)* Miss Olson!

MISS OLSON: *(Calmly)* . . . I didn't know it was so easy, I said to him. . . .

SISTER KARIN: *(Yelling)* Please, Miss Olson! I can see that you can do it. Come back! I believe you. I believe you.[23]

This is the symbolic triumph of the weak over the strong and an assertion of the weaker's right to his or her own world, well before Milos Forman's film of Ken Kesey's *One flew over the cuckoo's nest* enlisted massive support for psychiatric patients.

Yet another variant of invisibility is found in *Demonstranten* [The Demonstrator, 1969], which opens with a collage of voices commenting on an occurrence of some kind. Sound effects suggest locations such as a rush-hour street, a train, a busy office, a park bench; clearly a youth is in trouble. His parents discuss his disappearance. The father has searched for him all night and swears to wring his neck. The situation is evidently not new: "He turns us into laughing stocks in the whole district!"[24] His son Jerry's voice is heard next, explaining that he simply had to leave the workmen's hut where he was sitting with his father and workmates, he could hardly breathe. Something impelled him to walk into town in the rapidly falling dusk, he heard a voice calling him and he climbed up onto the roof of a tall building to get nearer to it. Bystanders now voice their reactions: "He's some kind of demonstrator of course. I've got a nephew who's just the same. . . . Maybe he's soft in the head. . . . A good thing, at least, that he goes behind the chimney to relieve himself,"[25] and so on. When his father starts to climb up, Jerry threatens to jump. Three days later, he prepares to descend. But as he pauses at the top of the fire escape, in full view of the spectators, he vanishes from sight. The closing words are his, as he describes a large hand lifting him up into the sky: ". . . it had cleared and stopped raining. . . . Something lifted me slowly up. . . . I saw the fire escape and the roof slowly sink down below me, I saw some people waiting in the street below. . . . Suddenly it wasn't hard to breathe any longer. Nobody was hollering either, I was weightless, weightless . . . I floated . . . I was a butterfly. . . ."[26] Just as Miss Olson walks off across the water, so Jerry floats up into the sky and leaves his failures behind him. There is no mistaking this as dream fulfilment, the sole recourse of the powerless. It acts as a poetic and antithetical counterpart to the ominous short story "The Father" in *Close Relations,* in which exactly the same situation arises. For there the father sucks his pipe comfortably and says: "Sure, the boy'll come down . . . he'll be flattened out of course, flat as a flounder, but he'll certainly be coming down one of these days . . ."(52).

The Myth of Wu Tao-Tzu once more. It seems fitting to round off this sample of Evander's radio plays with his latest to date, commissioned for a series commemorating C. J. L. Almqvist (1793– 1866), one of Sweden's most imaginative and enigmatic writers.[27] An ardent romantic when young, he was for a time Sweden's most widely read author. Although ordained, he became increasingly radical in his social views and shocked his public by advocating marriages of conscience rather than the fetters of institutionalized wedlock. Having put himself beyond the pale with the Establishment, he was finally accused of the attempted poisoning of a moneylender. He fled to the United States, where he married bigamously and lived under an assumed name in Philadelphia. Homesickness finally impelled him to return to Europe, old and sick, and he died in Germany in 1866 while still hoping to return to his beloved Sweden.

Evander's play, *Det är redan mörkt, Horst Müller måste väckas* [It's already dark, it's time to wake Horst Müller, 1973], shows us Almqvist in Germany shortly before his death. Under the name of Horst Müller and occupied with painting, he lives as the paying guest of a kindly bookseller's wife. He has two striking characteristics: he works by nocturnal candlelight and is in the habit of inviting his hostess and her guests to join with him in prayer (a reminder of Almqvist's pietistic leanings): "Heavenly father, almighty God, listen to the need in our hearts! . . . Turn to us in our sinful ways, and guide us in our endless foolishness! . . . Turn also to all who are consumed by the unfathomable pain of remorse . . . as you have already turned to those whose sins have been forgiven. . . . and let your light shine upon us and prepare us for your great eternity."[28] The climax occurs when the town's police inspector (suspicious of the mysterious foreigner), an art critic, the landlady, and her daughter, assemble at dusk to see Horst Müller unveil a large painting in the attic. When Müller removes the dustsheet, a gasp goes up as the whole room is illuminated by the glowing summer scene on the canvas.

BOOKSELLER'S WIFE: I seem to recognize the landscape . . . as though I had been here before. . . . It's unbelievable, Herr Müller, one can feel the warmth and the scents of summer. . . .

MÜLLER: You can come closer. . . .

(Gradually the outdoor atmosphere is magnified, significant sounds from the summer landscape.)[29]

All present—with the exception of the art critic, who stays outside and urges them to behave like educated people—enter the painting, irresistibly drawn by the shimmering Swedish landscape.

Here, for the second time in Evander's work, an artist steps inside his landscape (Forsberg in *The Upstarts* was the first to do so, as we have recently had occasion to recall). What is more, his audience joins him. This is not only an inspired figurative reflection of the fact that the tragic enigma Almqvist now, a century after his death, has left the sad and squalid realities of his life far behind him. It also proclaims the belief, seven years after the appearance of Sven Lindqvist's *Myten om Wu Tao-tzu*, that art has magical properties which no amount of documentaries can substitute for. When the bookseller's wife moves into the enchanted landscape, she exclaims, "But it's all quite unbelievable. How has it been possible to paint like this, won't you explain it to us, Herr Müller? How is it possible?" and the painter replies that he does not know, except that "I have had an eye for human beings and their condition. . . . I have had an eye for human beings. . . ."[30] His words, a direct quotation from Almqvist,[31] tell us that the feat builds neither on facts nor figures nor arguments, but on a gift for seeing into people's hearts and then visibly recreating their hopes and longings. That Horst Müller also spoke for his own creator's aesthetic, there can be little doubt.

Evander's radio plays have been performed in Norway, Finland, Denmark, West Germany, Poland, Italy, and Canada. But since 1973, when he wrote about Horst Müller, television has come to replace radio as his chosen medium for drama. "I have been commissioned to write my fourteenth play for the Radio Theater, but I don't feel particularly attracted," he wrote in 1978, "I believe the medium in a way is a transitional stage."[32]

Stage plays

All the days of my life.   Evander's first stage play—*Och alla min levnads dagar* [All the days of my life, 1972]—was commissioned by the Royal Dramatic Theater in Stockholm, but actually had its premiere in Gothenburg, where it was an unqualified success.

The setting is a slightly seedy boardinghouse at the end of the seaside holiday season. We cannot do better than allow the drama critic of *Dagens Nyheter* to describe the situation:

Naturally, there is trivial small talk. Naturally, there are magnified existential lies. Naturally, there are unsuccessful feelers for contact. Naturally, there is a mysterious individual whom we never see, but whom everybody talks about.

Naturally, the majority of the guests are revealed as being mentally unwell. One of them suffers from agoraphobia and dares not leave the house. Another one, a schoolmaster, is as pathologically querulous as his daily paper, Svenska Dagbladet. This boardinghouse is more or less a sort of convalescent home for the emotionally handicapped. The guests detest it, but they keep returning. At least there is a community feeling there.

Naturally this is literary kitsch. But what does it matter when Evander's dialogue transforms it all into sensitive and living theater? He can express the clumsy and the awkwardly uncouth. He can express exploding fury as well as perfect cynicism. He is amusing and witty, and as swift as a weasel when he slips into pathos.

For he also dares to be pathetic. . . . In a few scenes, a couple of the characters bare their inner nerve centers of fear and anguish. Their despair suddenly becomes your own, as you sit there in the auditorium.[33]

Another critic found something Chechovian about the minimal action of the play and its cluster of people about to be scattered, "their irresponsibility and helplessness, their gullibility and blindness, transposed and translated into the welfare state."[34] But the Chechov association is accidental, for Evander never had him in mind when writing his play.[35] Rather, he seems to have placed characters from some of his novels on the stage. The hypochondriac Werner is a close relation of Axel Schröder in *Foreman Lundin:* "The whole area round my heart is populated by dangerous insects. Every morning when I wake, I lie a while and wait for a signal from them,"[36] he tells the kindly proprietress. "What does the doctor say?" "Nothing." "And what do you say?" "That I feel a terrible anxiety."[37] As for the sarcastic and intolerant schoolmaster Marcus, he is related to the physics master with the sorrowful eyes. When a harmless married couple argue about somebody's correct surname, Marcus, as though addressing pupils, describes the astronomical distances of the universe:

MARCUS: One hundred million earths with an average of two billion beings, again a conservative estimate. . . . Let us say two hundred million billion beings. And out of these you sit arguing about whether one single specimen is called Johnson or Johanson. You must agree, it's too damnable! *(Short pause)*
EJNAR: There's something about your reasoning that I don't care for.
MARCUS: I'll be polite enough not to pursue that any further.
EJNAR: What do you mean by that?
MARCUS: I mean that people as a rule dislike what they don't understand.[38]

Yet symptomatically, it is precisely Marcus who has not had a good word to say to or of his fellow guests and the boardinghouse, who is found sitting in the lounge after the last bus has gone and the place is being closed up—crying.

It is a deeply moving curtain.

The Goldfish.   The family in *Guldfiskarna* [The Goldfish, 1975] lives in accommodation provided by the brickworks at which the father and his two sons work—an environment familiar to us from the novel *Foreman Lundin*. The father and his elder son, Martin, have both ruined their backs laboring, but are loyal to the works. Henry, the younger son, is a Marxist awaiting the imminent collapse of capitalism and its triumphant replacement by a socialist state. There is also a long-term guest, the hypochondriac Waldemar. "You show your cards openly," Martin says to him, "you don't try to pass yourself off as anything but an idler who lies on the sofa all day. . . . That's what I call an honest idler! Who doesn't pull his weight, but who doesn't either con others into believing that he does!"[39] Then, turning

to Henry, who takes time off from work in order to agitate among his
fellow workers, "Or maybe you think that what I've been saying is
just capitalist clap-trap?" "I can't deny that you always make a better
impression when you keep your mouth shut,"[40] comes the amiable
reply.

Their mother's views are inconsistent. On the one hand she senses
that a crisis is brewing at the works and she blames her husband and
Martin for not facing the fact squarely—indeed, she compares them to
goldfish she recollects from her childhood, who would bury their
heads in the sand whenever anyone approached. On the other hand,
she answers her younger son's political pronouncements by pointing
out how lucky they are to have a low rent and the amenities offered by
the works owner.

Finally, there is the sixteen-year-old daughter who is dreamy and
artistic and who Evander says he intended as a contrast to the political
and social issues raised by the other protagonists.[41]

The humor of this comedy (for it was published together with *All
the days of my life* under the collective title *Two Comedies*) resides in
repartee rather than comic action. Waldemar trots out stock phrases
(recognizable as echoes from a youth in *The Physics Master's
Sorrowful Eyes*) such as the gobbledygook "as for that concomitancy,
there's no concatenation in that cohabitation."[42] And his hypochondria
leads him to repeat that his days are numbered and that he has no
pulse any longer. The good-natured father counters this by observing
that "Waldemar doesn't need a doctor. What he needs is a theater
critic,"[43] and his wife reports after the doctor has been that he "hadn't
met a healthier person since he talked to Waldemar last time."[44] Not
even the news that the works are to be closed down and that
Waldemar ends up by hanging himself in the belief that the family
will be unable to give him a home any longer, turns this comedy into
a tragedy. Not that the play makes light of human problems, but the
basically reassuring family circle which absorbs—and indeed thrives
on—temperamental differences is *entertaining* in the same way that a
television series is. (The B.B.C.'s *The Forsythe Saga* and *The Brothers*
had been longrunning exponents of the genre on Swedish Television.)
The comparison is strengthened by the feeling that each one of the
play's five scenes would stand nicely on its own, providing appropriate

portions of food for thought and laughter, a spice of excitement in a meeting between a pair of ex-lovers, and, above all, that indefinable feeling of being present in somebody's home, partaking of their everyday life, which is the hallmark of the small screen's entertainment. The likeness is reinforced by the play's straightforwardly realistic mode which lacks the symbolic and mysterious elements found in Evander's radio plays.

The Goldfish reflects the topical issue of industrial closure and its social effects by means of a mixture of two resigned conformists (father and elder son), one revolutionary (younger son), and one social critic (mother) grateful for small mercies. This balance of attitudes precludes any political message other than an obvious dislike of the negative aspects of capitalism. So it is easy to understand that the producer of the Gothenburg performance, who had no eye for the play's existential aspects, reacted "like a ship-wrecked Marxist," clinging onto the debris of whatever social criticism he could find in the waves, to quote a witty reviewer.[45] That the work's political and existentialist aspects should pull in different directions is not surprising. It was, after all, commissioned by the Gothenburg City Theater, which had made a name for itself as a fosterer of radical group theater, whereas Evander's strength lies in his "having an eye for human beings"—to recall Almqvist's phrase—and their particular individual predicaments. A concrete link with Horst Müller/Almqvist is found in the touching prayer composed and read out by the young daughter after Valdermar's suicide, with phraseology strongly reminiscent of Müller's.

> Turn to poor little Waldemar
> and let your hands give him the warmth
> which he always hoped for as he lay on the sofa and shivered.
> Turn to Waldemar and welcome him into your kingdom.
> Turn to us all
> now and in all life's stages,
> now and in the hour of our death,
> and let your merciful light shine upon us
> and prepare us for the great eternity
> which awaits us!
> Amen.[46]

This is, to date, Evander's latest stage play. More and more, he seems absorbed by the format of what we might call the chamber television film, perhaps more suited to his temperament and style than full-length stage plays.

Television films

Evander's television films share with his radio plays a sensitivity and gentle melancholy which eschew glossiness and pure entertainment. A brief presentation of some of these films—all written and directed by Evander—will serve to indicate their particular qualities.

Plötsligt medan Harry levde [Suddenly, while Harry was alive, 1971] shows us a lonely, retired railway worker, Sigfrid. His wife has left him, and when his son Harry dies, he regards it as another desertion, particularly when Harry's girl friend refuses to come and look after him. In addition, his only friend lets him down. Why? We only know that Sigfrid has never had the ability to listen to and identify with other people.

It is a simple, slow-moving story, which ends with the old man staring bitterly out of the window, to the commentator's words: ". . . he will never understand who or what has built the invisible walls which have turned him into an utterly lonely person in this life and world, which he was once born to love."[47] There is an entirely convincing awkwardness and triviality in the way the characters, mostly played by amateur actors, speak to each other. The atmosphere distilled is one of emotional deprivation in the midst of the welfare state. The following year, Evander shot *Resan från Främlingshem* [The Journey from Strangers Haven, 1972] in a real village (Främlingshem) in his native Gästrikland, using the formula of a countdown to death, which had been so successful in *The Last Day of Valle Hedman's Life*. The elegiac beauty of the autumn landscape fills the screen as seven passengers board a country bus for what will be the last journey of their lives, for in twenty minutes' time the bus will be demolished by a train at a level crossing. We see seven human beings, each one with his or her own concerns uppermost in mind, reserved and self-absorbed, utterly unaware that the gift of life is about to be taken from them.

We have already noted the dialectical presentation of an identical father-son conflict, first in a short story showing the father confident of victory, then in a radio play with the son as the symbolic victor who vanishes into thin air. Evander provided yet another—reconciliatory—resolution to the theme in his televison film *Återkomsten* [The Return, 1976]. In essence it is based on a short story of his, in which a man sets out to track someone down in a murderous rage.[48] When he finally suceeds in finding him by bursting into the room where he is sleeping, we expect him to commit mindless violence. But the object of his pursuit sits quietly up in bed, and the pursuer falls to his knees, throws his arms around the young man's waist, and sobs as though his heart would break. "Don't cry, Dad," says the young man gently.[49] In the television version, a farmer's heartless treatment of those nearest to him has its origins in his bitterness at his only son having left home. When he at last finds his son again, the layers of hard protective armoring fall off him, and he ends up "in a sort of pietá in reverse,"[50] weeping in his son's lap. In a magazine article referring to this film, Evander wrote that one of his primary aims in the field of television and fiction is to examine what it is that causes our incurable contempt for everything connected with failure, what or who it is that so early impells us to side against what is incomplete and unsuccessful, to worship courage and strength, while turning our backs on the person being vanquished. "Even if you cannot 'get at' the causes, I still think it is meaningful to try to present and describe the symptoms, then you will at least have gone some little way toward establishing a diagnosis,"[51] he maintained.

Evander's next major film was *Fusket* [Cheating, 1978]. He wrote it for two outstanding Swedish actors, Anders Ek and Hans Alfredson,[52] who—as an artist and a roof layer respectively—meet in an unheated summer cottage one cold winter's afternoon in order to commit a planned joint suicide. The film develops into a contest of wills, about which there is something very Strindbergian; we need only think of *Creditors, The Stronger*, and *Pariah*. But this piece has its own personal tone and climax.

The two men scarcely know each other, but they have this in common—neither of them thinks life is worth living; the artist, because he has reached an age when he can anticipate everything that is going to happen to him, and the roof layer, because he is lonely since his wife died, and plagued by rheumatism and thirst for strong drink. The painter places a pistol on the table, and they sit talking before putting their plan into effect. At this point there is an unexpected knock on the door. It is Katarina, a neighboring housewife, who has noticed that there is someone in the normally empty cottage. She invites them to come across for a cup of coffee whenever they feel like it, and the roof layer says that she will be seeing them. When the artist later taxes him for this remark, he retorts that he feels like a hot drink, and anyway, she reminds him of his deceased wife. It begins to be apparent that a battle is under way.

The artist says that despite lack of worldly success he has always tried faithfully to follow his inner voice: "The worst thing that ever happened to me was when someone accused me of cheating. Of not being true to my own intentions but only painting the way I thought people wanted me to, of not being true to myself."[53] The roof layer agrees that this is the worst one can be accused of—and that a good many in his line also cheat, but not those who take their work seriously.

The artist now thinks it is time for them to do what they have met for, but the roof layer wants a cup of coffee and suggests waiting until tomorrow. Who knows? Something really nice might happen that very evening—a commission for a huge painting, for instance. Despite the artist's accusation that he is cheating and failing a friend, the roof layer insists that he is only speaking about today, in the same way as members of Alcoholics Anonymous do not say they will never drink again, just that they will not drink one day at a time. If his friend were a good artist and had "an eye for human beings and their condition,"[54] as he claims to have, he would realize that the roof layer needed a cup of coffee.

The artist knows exactly why he wishes to commit suicide, and no arguments to the contrary can deflect him, but he has an irrational weakness—he cannot take the step on his own, he needs a companion. So despite his protests, the last image is of the roof layer with an arm around his unwilling shoulders, leading him across to the neighbors for a hot drink and the warmth of human companionship.

Life's simple, basic values are confirmed. They are ultimately stronger than the artist's pride and the manual worker's pain-wracked joints and loneliness. There are levels of cheating: cheating our own counsels of despair is infinitely preferable to cheating ourselves of life's infinite capacity for unexpected consolation.

Evander's latest television film to date is *Den ynkryggen Valdemar* [That poor wretch Waldemar, 1980]. Made with a distinguished cast,[55] it builds on a conflict between a patient and hospital staff. The patient is a writer, whose lack of self-confidence is compensated for by prickly arrogance, while the well-meaning psychotherapist represents repressive tolerance at its most amiable. The absurd and miraculous climax shows the patient willing himself to dissolve into thin air, to become *invisible*—much to the psychotherapist's horror—as the only logical response to the way he is being treated.

Although it is not possible to ascribe Evander's view of mental illness directly to the writings of R. D. Laing and David Cooper, he sympathizes with what he takes to be their negative attitude to traditional psychiatric methods as demonstrated respectively in Ken Loach's film *Family Life,* based on Laing's *The Politics of the Family,*[56] and David Cooper's *The Death of the Family,*[57] and, like them, he tends to regard patients' behavior as a strategy to counter intolerable pressures exerted by the environment.

Drama as an outlet for mysticism

It will have become apparent in this study that Evander has had to use a good deal of ingenuity as a novelist to combine his personal vision and experience with the constraints imposed on fiction by the canons of literature established by the radical consensus of the 1960s and 1970s. The poetic side of his talent, his propensity to invest objects and attitudes of everyday life with heightened significance, has found an outlet in his dramatic works. His creative imagination evidently thrives in a medium which not only tolerates but encourages fantasy and symbolism.

His radio plays and films are easily recognizable with their characteristic thematic composition and undertones of tragic melancholy. It is not his method to concentrate on a psychological portrait of a single individual, nor on a plot or story for its own sake. Instead, he presents relationships and situations. His people are demonstrably dependent on each other—for good or ill. His parents and children, lonely youngsters, hypochondriacs, bullies, and dreamers, are all existentially vulnerable and in need of reassurance. The ones who are most sorely tried have an ultimate resource—they can partake of the miraculous. They walk on water, step inside paintings, and vanish into thin air. Their reality suddenly transcends normal boundaries. They demonstrate that their author is both realist and mystic.

Chapter Six
Conclusion

Formalism

The author as magician. Evander's books are frequently characterized by the problematic status of the information they offer. The narrator may introduce himself as Per Gunnar Evander and provide corroborative factual evidence of identity (i.e., in *Dear Mr. Evander*, *The Upstarts*, *A Love Story*, and *The Story of Joseph*), only to spin a fictitious web out of this thread. This method of presenting the first person narrator as being identical with the author Per Gunnar Evander, down to factual details of his work at the Radio Corporation and the introduction into the narrative of indisputably real and publicly known colleagues (e.g., the film photographer Bengt Åke Kimbré and the radio producer Gunnar Balgård),[1] has inevitably invited speculation about the veracity or otherwise of the situations set up in these books and even charges of role-playing and mystification. Evander would of course answer that his books are true at a deeper level than that of a trivial correspondence to appearances, in the sense in which a work of art is true or false in essence rather than in facticity. But the question still remains why he so often and with such intensity seeks to imbue his fiction with verisimilitude and in particular why he adopts the stance of actual participant in his own novels.

The first thing to note is that he has not been alone in the latter practice. Sven Delblanc in *Nattressa [Journey at night,* 1967], P. O. Enquist in *The Legionnaires* (1968), and Lars Gustafsson in *Herr Gustafsson själv* [Mr. Gustafsson himself, 1971] also appear as themselves in their own books. The documentary mode, we need to recall, strove to present facts objectively (albeit selectively) and to keep close to empirical reality (weighted toward social and economic factors). It was a reaction against the traditional novel of illusion which creates a fictional world and persuades the reader to suspend disbelief. The fictional world is ruled over by an all-powerful magician, the invisible yet omnipresent narrator. For this reason, writers who in the politicized climate of the late 1960s shared the prevalent distrust of pure art or literature, appeared in their own books in the role of anticonjurers, saying in effect, "Look, this is how it is done. There's no magic about these words of mine, I am a human being just like the rest of you."

It is the contention of this study that Evander is basically a magician. He delights in creating the literary equivalent of the visual artist's *trompe l'oeil*. When he appears in his books in person it is not in order to undermine the power of fiction but to exploit it. When he as narrator supplies himself with the incontrovertible persona of Per Gunnar Evander, this appears to distance him from characters with whom he, psychologically speaking, is closely identified. It enables him to analyze Hadar Forsberg and kid brother Henning, just as a parallel phenomenon enables the psychotherapist — the author in another guise—to confront his eponymous patient Lillemor Holm. We could add that in *The Story of Joseph* he makes a show of subverting his own fiction by expatiating in the person of Per Gunnar Evander on the difficulties of writing it. But the real themes of the book are involuntary violence, guilt, and fear, not the problematics of the metanovel. Contrary to its formal properties of a "workshop" product, that novel does *not*, in terms of our metaphor, show us how the card trick works and where the false bottom is located.

Simulated ignorance and inculcated doubt. Another feature of Evander's prose, linked to documentary, is simulated ignorance. The magician naturally has all the answers to the world he has created, whereas the objective writer-as-observer is aware of gaps in his knowledge. Once again, Evander in the role of the former adopts the manner of the latter. In the following extract from *Mondays with Fanny*, having first established unequivocally that a man has fetched his elderly mother for a Sunday drive, he then proceeds to hedge his account with tentative formulations as though he were not the originator of his own fiction: "*Maybe* his mother anyway says something about the weather, *maybe* she says something about the unexpected thaw . . . and *maybe* Egon Backman explains that he has just washed the car . . . she *probably* complains that the car is too cramped. . . . It is *highly likely* that his mother protests about seatbelts and *no doubt* Backman is prepared . . ." (14; my italics).

The technique is reminiscent of that of P. O. Sundman, whose detached, behavioristic narrative style, as we have already noted, greatly influenced Evander's early work, with the important distinction that Evander's ambiguities are not anchored in epistemological uncertainty about the nature of reality and what human beings can and cannot know, whereas Sundman's are. Sundman has written of himself that the basis of his technique lies in confining his narrative to external occurrences and abstaining from the construction of a psychological "inner course of events" for his characters. He goes on to say that one "cannot acquire certain knowledge about others 'through oneself,' we are too different," adding, "Our fellow human beings are inaccessible as individuals. Spending time together, conversations, and testimony broaden our knowledge, but provide no definitive certainty in individual cases."[2] Evander, on the other hand, believes that one *can* come to understand one's fellowmen, as his psychological analysis of the main characters in his books has increasingly shown: "I believe we can know infinitely more about ourselves and infinitely more about each other."[3]

So we find that underneath a formal stance normally in literature associated with skepticism and detachment there beats in Evander's novels the strong pulse of a belief in the unique value of people's subjective experiences. How, then, is his manipulatory inculcation of doubt to be explained? Inducing uncertainty is a useful training in not swallowing the pronouncements of people in authority, the media, and politicians, was an answer he gave in 1977.[4] We can also fall back on something he wrote in his twenties: "in a way I feel a strange confidence in states of uncertainty and fragility, in injuries which need comfort in order to heal. In fact, this seems to be the only thing which unequivocally makes people realize how immeasurably they depend upon each other, how enormously they need each other."[5]

Structural polarities.   Evander does not present character studies, he demonstrates existential dilemmas, frequently by means of antithetical pairs. Foreman Lundin and Axel Schröder (*Foreman Lundin*), Per Gunnar and his brother Henning (*A Love Story*), the teacher and his son (*The Physics Master's Sorrowful Eyes*), the Sole and Lillemor Holm (*The Case of Lillemor Holm*), are all cases in point. Sometimes the conflict is illustrated by tensions within a single individual—and here Jimmy (*The Last Adventure*), Robert (*Mondays with Fanny*), and Richard (*Earth Divine*) are obvious examples. It could be argued that the transition from reality to mysticism—as exemplified at the close of *Dear Mr. Evander, The Physics Master's Sorrowful Eyes* and *The Upstarts*—reflects the same dichotomous principle—polarities in search of redeeming syntheses.

The message

While Evander's narrative modes have varied, his concerns have been constant. Whether by means of the absurdistic allegory in *Close Relations*, the detached documentary of *The Upstarts*, the metanovel approach of *The Story of Joseph*, or the poetic fantasy of his radio plays, his message is that human beings are in need of comfort and relationships based on trust and self-respect. We have to recognize how our own past has shaped us, and we have to take responsibility for how we ourselves treat others. There is nothing novel about this message. What is compelling is the urgency with which Evander develops his themes. Secular Christianity would be a way of describing them.

The steadfast loner

Evander has built up a formidable position as a writer, but he is personally reticent. He is not a public debater or pundit. Apart from an occasional feature program on radio or television, he is a private person who speaks through his works. There may be one or two more strikingly intellectual writers than he in his generation, but none has been more consistently and unopportunistically "faithful to his own *Angst*," to borrow a phrase once applied to Stig Dagerman.[6] He has sometimes adopted a chameleonlike camouflage appropriate to prevailing literary trends. But no other Swedish writer today is so concerned to convey what it feels like to live with the weight of personal insecurity and existential pain, or is so hopeful against all the odds about the possibility of overcoming them.

Notes and References

Abbreviations

AB	*Aftonbladet*
Arbt	*Arbetet*
BLM	*Bonniers Litterära Magasin*
DN	*Dagens Nyheter*
Expr	*Expressen*
GefleD	*Gefle Dagblad*
GHT	*Göteborgs Handels-och Sjöfartstidning*
GP	*Göteborgs-Posten*
SDS	*Sydsvenska Dagbladet Snällposten*
SRP	*Svenska radiopjäser (Sveriges Radios förlag, Stockholm)*
SvD	*Svenska Dagbladet*
VJ	*Vecko-Journalen*

Preface

1. P. O. Enquist, *The Legionnaires: a documentary novel*, trans. Alan Blair (New York: Delacorte Press/Seymour Lawrence, 1974), p. 31.
2. Matts Rying, "Fredagarna med Hr Evander," in *Ditt okända förflutna. En vänbok till Erik Hj. Linder* (Stockholm, 1976), pp. 179–195.

Chapter One

1. Evander, *Uppkomlingarna—en personundersökning* (Stockholm, 1969), p.37.
2. Evander, *En kärleksroman* (Stockholm, 1971), p. 150.
3. Cf. Rying, pp. 179–80.
4. Cf. Carl-Olof Lång, "Per Gunnar Evander: Var stor i orden lilla du!" *VJ* 26 (1979): 8.
5. "Mitt porträtt av mig," *Vi* 6 (1976): 10–11.
6. Ibid., p. 11.
7. Rying, pp. 180–81.

8. The phrase "typical schoolmaster" was used by Evander in conversation with the author. This correcting and collecting solecisms is recalled by Evander's friend Göran Norström.

9. In conversation with the author.

10. "Mitt porträtt av mig," p. 11.

11. Ibid., p. 10.

12. Johannes Larsson, "Per Gunnar Evander, 41," AB, 23 September 1974.

13. Elisabeth Sörenson, "Inte enbart författare," SvD, 19 January 1975.

14. Letter to the author dated June 1980.

15. "Stockholmsbilen" by Stig Dagerman, with commentary "Jag kände igen mina egna villkor" by Evander, in DN, 20 August 1977.

16. "Mitt porträtt av mig," pp. 10–11.

17. In conversation with the author.

18. In a letter to the author, Evander writes, in June 1980, "Perhaps you can glean something more about my biography when you read Fear's Dwelling Place" (proofs of which he sent). The passage quoted (p. 206 in the novel) is the most obvious example of autobiographical material.

19. Margareta Romdahl, "Per Gunnar Evander—Författaren och TV—producenten," DN, 13 July 1970.

20. In conversation with the author.

21. Rying, p. 183.

22. Nils Gunnar Nilsson, "Är även Judas värd vår medkänsla?" SDS, 13 August 1978.

23. In conversation with the author. Also in Rying, p. 182.

24. Cf. Torben Broström, Modern svensk litteratur (Stockholm: Bonniers, 1974), pp. 100–107 and Lars Gustafsson, The Public Dialogue in Sweden (Stockholm: Norstedts, 1964), pp. 36–44.

25. Barabbas, trans. Alan Blair (New York: Random House, 1951). Note also the monograph on Pär Lagerkvist by Robert Spector (Boston: Twayne Publishers, 1973).

26. Nihilistiskt credo (Stockholm, 1964), p. 95. There is a monograph on Lars Gyllensten by Hans Isaksson (Boston: Twayne Publishers, 1978).

27. Göran Palm, "Blir vi förda bakom ljuset?" Expr, 22 June 1965.

28. The Peruvian organizer of rural workers, Hugo Blanco, who spent some years of exile in Sweden during the late 1960s, familiarized Swedes with the concept of concienciatización, and Jan Myrdal in particular stressed the need for political awareness in his series of miscellaneous writings Skriftställning (Stockholm, 1968–).

29. Sven Delblanc, Åsnebrygga (Stockholm: Bonniers, 1969), p. 129.

30. P. O. Sundman, *The Flight of the 'Eagle': a documentary novel,* trans. Mary Sandbach (London: Secker & Warburg, 1970).

31. *Linjer i nordisk prosa. Sverige 1965–1975,* ed. Kjerstin Norén (Lund: Bo Cavefors, 1977), p. 34.

32. N. G. Nilsson, "Vi måste lära oss mera om döden," *SDS,* 21 May 1972.

33. Bengt Holmqvist, "Ett ord säger mer än tusen bilder," *DN,* 2 October 1970.

34. Hjalmar Bergman, *God's Orchid,* trans. E. Classen (Copenhagen: Gyldendal, 1924).

35. "Att vara författare är ett helvete," *Expr,* 24 October 1969.

36. *BLM* 6 (1979): 378.

Chapter Two

1. The stories in *Evil Tales* are included in Pär Lagerkvist's *The Marriage Feast and other stories,* trans. Alan Blair (London: Chatto & Windus, 1955).

2. St. John 19:21–22: "Then said the chief priests of the Jews to Pilate, Write not, the King of the Jews; but that he said, I am King of the Jews. Pilate answered, What I have written I have written."

3. Cf. Peter Ortman, "Hadar Forsberg i verkligheten," *SDS,* 5 September 1969: "It's as though Evander's fictional characters become aware of everyday reality, normally so impenetrable, cracking open and allowing them a glimpse into another world, that of mystic experience."

4. E. Hj. Linder, "Bäste herr Evander!" *GHT,* 25 August 1967.

5. Lars-Olof Franzén, "På flyktens villkor," *DN,* 25 August 1967.

6. The device of the telephone call as the agent of conscience featured prominently in Muriel Spark's *Memento mori* (London: Macmillan, 1959), but Evander was not familiar with this work.

7. In conversation with the author.

8. Göran Norström, "Slut med folkhögskolan?" *Expr,* 2 October 1968 and Evander's reply, "Bort med svärmeriet!" *Expr,* 14 October 1968.

9. A case in point would be the author Lars Ahlin, for whom two years at a folk high school constituted a turning-point from youthful vagrancy to dedicated literary work. See T. Lundell's *Lars Ahlin* (Boston: Twayne Publishers, 1978).

10. In conversation with the author.

11. "P. O. Enquist om en ny roman av Per Gunnar Evander," *Expr,* 1 October 1968.

12. Ibid.

13. Conversation with the author.

14. "Bort med svärmeriet!" *Expr,* 14 October 1968.

Chapter Three

1. E. Hj. Linder is the only reviewer to have observed this possibility. He writes in "Tortyr i källarvåningen," *GP,* 5 September 1969: "These diary notes, which some meddling investigator takes such pains over, could quite well be made up. They are—or could be—the novel! They are the sort of literary composition which involves enduring one's own failings and crimes."

2. P. O. Enquist, "Alla barnen i Hadar Forsbergs källare," *Expr,* 5 September 1969.

3. E.g., L. Frick, "Evanders personundersökning," *Arbetaren,* 14 November 1969; B. Nilsson, "Per Gunnar Evander—en av de bästa författarna här i landet," *Böckernas värld* 4 (1971): 96; B. Tunander, "Den bedrägliga verkligheten," *DN,* 27 October 1969.

4. Evander has confirmed to the author in conversation that the American names were designed as an association to Vietnam.

5. According to Greek mythology Rhadamanthus, one of the judges of the underworld, excelled in severe and just punishments. It might, in addition, be supposed that Evander had in mind the Swedish mystic Emanuel Swedenborg's idea of a Hell precisely equivalent to the type of sin committed, but he disclaims this.

6. Quoted from Vergil, *The Aeneid,* trans. W. F. Jackson Knight (London: Penguin Books, 1963), p. 169.

7. Hermann Hesse, "Life story briefly told" (1925), in *Autobiographical Writings,* ed. Theodore Ziolkowski (London: Cape, 1973), pp. 43–62.

8. S. Lindqvist, *Slagskuggan* (Stockholm: Bonniers, 1969) and *Jord och makt* (Stockholm: Bonniers, 1973).

9. "Något av ett svindlande äventyr," *GHT,* 5 June 1971.

10. Romdahl, *DN,* 13 July 1970.

11. See P. O. Enquist, "Schröder hette en fotograf . . . ," *Expr,* 2 October 1970.

12. For Almqvist's phrase, cf. chapter 5, note 31.

13. For Evander's irritation with the cliché "visual flair" (*bildsinne*) see "Varför inte dokumentär?" *DN,* 2 October 1970.

14. For an interesting interpretation of the film, "There was a kitchen with many photographs," see Nilsson, pp. 93–94.

15. "Jag har själv upplevt kroppsarbetets villkor," *DN*, 24 January 1971.

16. B. Holmqvist, "Ett ord säger mer än tusen bilder," *DN*, 2 October 1970.

17. "Varför inte dokumentärt?" *DN*, 2 October 1970.

18. *GHT*, 5 June 1971.

19. Three prize-winning entries, "Kritikertävlingens resultat," *GHT*, 3 June 1971.

20. Cf. transcript of the Swedish Broadcasting Corporation's program *Bokfönstret*, 17 November 1971, p. 1.

21. E.g., A. Pleijel, "Uppmärksam kärlekshistoria," *AB*, 22 October 1971; K. Sundén, "En ny roman av Per Gunnar Evander," *Expr*, 22 October 1971; I. Wizelius, "Bröder emellan," *DN*, 22 October 1971 ("Everything points to the brother, too, more or less completely being taken from real life"); K. E. Lagerlöf, "Per Gunnar Evander erövrar kärleken," *DN*, 18 February 1974.

22. *Bokfönstret*, p. 3.

23. Ibid., p. 3.

24. Notable examples of romantic anthropomorphism of migratory birds are found in the works of the nineteenth-century poets Tegnér, Stagnelius, and Runeberg.

25. Gun-Britt Sundström, *Maken* (Stockholm: Bonniers, 1976), p. 299.

26. In real life, Evander had been able, like Henning, to "see" hidden playing cards. The incident on pp. 162–63 of the novel is based on his own experience.

27. "Om tillståndet längtan," *DN*, 16 July 1971.

28. Ibid.

29. Karl Erik Lagerlöf, *Strömkantringens år och andra essäer om den nya litteraturen* (Stockholm: PAN/Norstedts, 1975), p. 18.

30. *DN*, 16 July 1971.

31. E.g., Åke Janzon, "I grunden är vi två," *SvD*, 22 October 1971; E. Hj. Linder, "Min bror är min spegel," *GP*, 10 November 1971.

32. E.g., A. Ringblom, "Om tillståndet längtan," *SDS*, 2 November 1971; B. Palmqvist, "Herr Evander och hans lillebror," *Arbt*, 23 October 1971.

33. In response to my query (based on reading the proofs of the novel), Evander replied on 12 July 1980 that "the two newspapers were *DN* and *Arbetet*. *DN* had not actually attacked me in this connection but I considered it big enough to cover for the others. Be that as it may—I had a good relationship with *DN* at the time; they published other things by me instead."

His fictionalized account in *Fear's Dwelling Place* is hence primarily interesting as a reflection of his violent reaction to slighting remarks by colleagues elsewhere than in *DN*.

34. Evander has told the author that there was a live model for Joseph, a worker from Bollnäs, committed to a psychiatric hospital in Borlänge.

35. Lars Gustafsson, "Evander: Han fastnar på vägen," *Expr*, 20 October 1972.

36. Sven Delblanc, "Evander och hans kritiker," *Expr*, 30 October 1972.

37. A prize deriving from the bequest of the painter Anders Zorn (1860–1920) to the Swedish Academy.

Chapter Four

1. See Rying, p. 184.

2. Evander has told me that the preliminary draft was actually written in the first person.

3. Rying, p. 194.

4. The citation appeared in Bonniers's press advertisements.

5. Evander confirms this interpretation in Rying, p. 188.

6. Gustaf Wingren, "En parentes av kärlek," *SDS*, 3 October 1974.

7. Ibid.

8. In conversation with the author.

9. "En svensk fasad berättar," *DN*, 26 September 1975.

10. Rying, pp. 193–94.

11. The title symbolizes the narrator's self-confessed tendency to retreat into her shell to avoid contact with other people.

12. Ruth Halldén, review of *Lungsnäckan*, *DN*, 21 January 1977.

13. Åke Leijonhufvud, review of *Lungsnäckan*, *SDS*, 21 January 1977.

14. Stenciled and hitherto unpublished interview by Matts Rying of the Swedish Broadcasting Corporation, p. 11, kindly placed at the author's disposal.

15. The myth of suicide as a Swedish sickness caused by the welfare state was propagated by President Eisenhower. A. Alvarez, in *The Savage God: A study of suicide* (London: Weidenfeld and Nicolson, 1971), p. 73, comments: "He seems to have been more than usually badly briefed. The present suicide-rate in Sweden is about the same as it was in 1910, before the social welfare schemes began. It is even lower than that of Switzerland, that haven of private enterprise and tax inducements, and is in fact ranked ninth on the most recent national suicide league table published by the World Health Organization."

16. When I questioned Evander on Henning's suicide, he admitted that it was narratively speaking convenient.

17. Evander's own interest in clairvoyance was reinforced by Olle Holmberg's *Den osannolika verkligheten* (Stockholm: Bonniers, 1968).

18. It is unclear whether Evander or his publishers worded the text.

19. Kerstin Vinterhed's interview with Evander, "Jag är inte Holm—jag kände henne," *DN*, 27 August 1977. Evander also informed me that Holm had changed her name two years earlier (thus neatly preventing anyone from consulting inquest records).

20. Karlis Branke, "Vårens debutanter," *VJ* 4 (1977): 30.

21. Åke Janzon, "Fallet Per Gunnar Evander," *SvD*, 26 August 1977.

22. Karlis Branke.

23. Lennart Frick, *New Swedish Books 1975–1978* (Stockholm, 1979), p. 26.

24. St. John 13:27. All Bible quotations in this chapter are taken from the Standard Revised version.

25. Isaiah 53:7.

26. Curt Jonasson, "Judas får upprättelse i ny Evander-roman," *SvD*, 15 April 1979.

27. Nils Gunnar Nilsson, "Är även Judas värd vår medkänsla?" *SDS*, 13 August 1978.

28. Ibid.

29. Ibid.

30. Ibid.

31. Ibid. Tor Hedberg, *Judas. En passionshistoria* (Stockholm: Bonniers, 1886); Eric Linklater, *Judas. A novel* (London: Jonathan Cape, 1939).

32. See Martha Larsson, "Judas äreräddad även i Italien," *SvD*, 10 July 1979.

33. See Kerstin Linder, " 'Josef'—ett verk av kärlek," *SvD*, 18 March 1979.

34. Already in the article "Förrädaren. Några reflexioner kring Judasgestalten," *GefleD*, 19 April 1962, Evander mentions the possibility of the name Iscariot being derived from "sicarius," although he observes that the fact that Judas's father is called Simon Iscariot speaks against the theory. He is also aware that philologists discount this etymological explanation nowadays. In spite of this, his imagination was stimulated by the idea of Judas as a man with revolutionary sympathies.

35. This theory is mentioned by Gunnar Hillerdal in *Jesu lärjungar* (Stockholm: Verbum, 1975), p. 84, which Evander used for background reading.

36. The original title was *Jesus, Gestalt und Geschichte* (Bern: Francke, 1957). Evander read the Swedish translation.

37. St. John 6:14–15

38. St. John 11:47–48

39. St. Matthew 10:8

40. Jonasson, *SvD,* 15 April 1979.

41. Ibid.

42. Bengt Holmqvist, "I gamla fotspår," *DN,* 25 January 1980.

43. *Gräv där du står. Hur man utforskar en arbetsplats.* (Stockholm: Bonniers, 1978).

44. I have written a fuller presentation of the problem in *BLM* 3 (June 1981), where I nevertheless stress that Evander has not commented on this dialectic to me and that my arguments must not be attributed to him, however self-evident I may find them.

45. Cf. Evander's television film "That poor wretch Waldemar" in chapter 5.

Chapter Five

1. E. Sörenson, *SvD* 19 January 1975.

2. In conversation with the author.

3. P. G. Engel and L. Janzon, *Sju decennier svensk teater under 1900–talet* (Stockholm, 1974), p. 196.

4. Sigvard Mårtensson, "Inledning," *SRP,* 1970, p. 510. Letter from Evander dated 14 September 1978.

6. C. O. Lång in conversation with the author.

7. *SRP,* 1966, p. 69.

8. Ibid., p. 70.

9. Ibid., p. 76.

10. Ibid., pp. 78–79.

11. Ibid., pp. 83–84.

12. Swedish Broadcasting Corporation (SBC) script of *Hadar skulle säkert förstå,* p. 49.

13. SBC script of *Inte ska du gråta,* p. 26.

14. Ibid., p. 27.

15. SBC script of *Överraskningen,* p. 57.

16. Ibid., final page.

17. *SRP,* 1970, p. 77.

18. Ibid., p. 76.

19. Ibid., p. 83.

20. Ibid., p. 99.

21. *SRP,* 1967, p. 58.

22. *SRP,* 1968, pp. 76–78.

23. Ibid., p. 79.

24. *SRP,* 1969, p. 16.

25. Ibid., pp. 28–29.

26. Ibid., pp. 37–38.

27. Cf. B. Romberg, *C. J. L. Almqvist* (Boston: Twayne Publishers, 1977).

28. *SRP,* 1973, pp. 46–47. (Interestingly, Evander has told me that the wording of this prayer was inspired by the notes of the Yngsjö murderer, Per Nilsson.

29. Ibid., p. 71.

30. Ibid., p. 73.

31. Almqvist's phrase (from "Det europeiska missnöjets grunder," in *Samlade skrifter,* imperial octave ed. [Stockholm: Bonniers, 1922], p. 70) also occurs obliquely in *Foreman Lundin,* p. 39 and in the short story version of Evander's television film "Cheating," in *Svenska noveller i TV* (Stockholm, 1978), pp. 75, 77.

32. Letter to the author dated 14 September 1978. Nevertheless, two new radio plays of his were broadcast in 1981: *Solkatten* and *Och sanningen skall göra eder fria.*

33. Bengt Jahnsson, "Evander i Göteborg—löftesrik scendebut," *DN,* 25 November 1972.

34. P. E. Wahlund on the play's revival in Stockholm, "Alla min levnads dagar. Dramatiska teatern," *SvD,* 10 March 1975.

35. In conversation with the author.

36. Evander, *Två radiopjäser,* p. 47.

37. Ibid., p. 50

38. Ibid., p. 73.

39. Ibid., p. 145.

40. Ibid., p. 146.

41. In conversation with the author.

42. Ibid., p. 157.

43. Ibid., p. 186.

44. Ibid., p. 190.

45. Leif Zern, "Doftlös version av 'Guldfiskarna,' " *DN,* 22 August 1975.

46. Evander, *Två komedier,* p. 257.

47. R. Nyberg, "TV i går," *AB,* 13 April 1971.

48. "Jag har det bäst som jag har det," *BLM* 3 (1972): 120–26.

49. Ibid. p. 126.

50. Åke Janzon, "Per Gunnar Evander när han är som bäst," *SvD*, 4 May 1976.

51. *TV Teatern. Maj 1976*. Internal duplicated SBC magazine, p. 13.

52. Anders Ek (1916–79), actor at the Royal Dramatic Theater. Hans Alfredson (b. 1928), entertainer and writer, well known for his collaboration with Tage Danielsson in the comic duo "HasseåTage."

53. SBC script, p. 38; See also *Svenska noveller i TV*, p. 75.

54. Ibid., pp. 42 and 77 respectively.

55. It was shot in April–May 1979 with Gunnel Broström, Ernst-Hugo Järegård, and Stig Järrel in the leading roles.

56. R. D. Laing, *The Politics of the Family* (London: Tavistock Publications Ltd, 1971).

57. David Cooper, *The Death of the Family* (London: Pelican Books, 1976).

Chapter Six

1. B. Å. Kimbré in *The Upstarts, A Love Story,* and *The Story of Joseph;* Gunnar Balgård in *A Love Story.*

2. Sundman's remarks are quoted in P. Hallberg's essay "Dokument-- engagemang—fiktion," *Nordisk tidskrift*, 1970, p. 89.

3. Rying, p. 187.

4. Ibid., p. 187.

5. "Brev hem," *Frihet* 7 (1959): 29.

6. The poet and critic Karl Vennberg in *Vi* 51–52 (1945), reviewing Stig Dagerman's novel *Ormen.* The English language lacks an exact equivalent to the Swedish term *ångest* (an indefinable state of anxiety). To existentialist thinkers a state of anxiety or dread is an inescapable part of human existence—and one which needs to be squarely faced.

Selected Bibliography

PRIMARY SOURCES

1. Novels

Bäste herr Evander [Dear Mr. Evander]. Stockholm: Bonniers, 1967. New paperback edition revised by the author, 1981.

Bäste herr Evander [Dear Mr. Evander]. Stockholm: Bonniers, 1967.

Det sista äventyret [The Last Adventure]. Stockholm: Bonniers, 1973. New hardback and first and second paperback editions, 1975. New paperback edition revised by the author, 1981.

Fallet Lillemor Holm [The Case of Lillemor Holm]. Stockholm: Bonniers, 1977. New paperback edition, 1979.

Fysiklärarens sorgsna ögon [The Physics Master's Sorrowful Eyes]. Stockholm: Bonniers, 1968.

Härlig är jorden [Earth Divine]. Stockholm; Bonniers, 1975. New hardback edition, 1977.

Judas Iskariots knutna händer]Judas Iscariot's Clenched Fists]. 1977.

Lungsnäckan [The Snail]. Stockholm: Bonniers, 1977. Under pseudonym Lillemor Holm.

Måndagarna med Fanny [Mondays with Fanny]. Stockholm: Bonniers, 1974. New paperback edition, 1975.

Se mig i mitt friska öga [Look Me in My Unblemished Eye]. Stockholm: Bonniers, 1980.

Sista dagen i Valle Hedmans liv [The Last Day of Valle Hedman's Life]. Stockholm: Författarförlaget, 1971. 2d ed., Stockholm: Bonniers, 1977.

Tegelmästare Lundin och stora världen [Foreman Lundin of the Brickworks and the Wide World]. Stockholm: Bonniers, 1970. New paperback edition, 1975.

Uppkomlingarna—en personundersökning [The Upstarts—An Investigation]. Stockholm: Bonniers, 1969. New paperback edition, 1974.

Ängslans boningar [Fear's Dwelling Place]. Stockholm: Bonniers, 1980. Paperback edition, Månpocket, 1981.

2. Short stories
Tjocka släkten [Close Relations]. Stockholm: Bonniers, 1965.

3. Stage plays
Två komedier [Two Comedies]. Stockholm: Norstedts, 1976. Contains *Och alla min levnads dagar* [All the days of my life] and *Guldfiskarna* [The Goldfish].

4. Radio plays (*Where a publisher is not indicated, the plays exist only as the Swedish Broadcasting Corporation's stenciled scripts*).
"*Demonstranten*" [The Demonstrator]. In *Svenska radiopjäser 1969*. Stockholm: Sveriges Radios Förlag, 1969. Pp. 11–38.
"Det är redan mörkt, Horst Müller måste väckas" [It's already dark, it's time to wake Horst Müller]. In *Svenska radiopjäser 1973*. Stockholm: Sveriges Radios Förlag, 1974. Pp. 37–73.
"Det är söndagseftermiddag, min bror springer på åkern" [It's Sunday afternoon and my brother's running across the field]. In *Svenska radiopjäser 1966*. Stockholm: Sveriges Radios Förlag, 1966. Pp. 65–84.
"Först trodde jag det var en fågel" [At first I thought it was a bird]. 1967
"Hadar skulle säkert förstå" [Hadar would be sure to understand]. 1966.
"I min ungdom speglade jag mig ofta" [In my young days I often looked at myself in the mirror]. In *Svenska radiopjäser 1970*. Stockholm: Sveriges Radios Förlag, 1970. Pp. 63–99.
"*Inte ska du gråta*" [There, there, don't cry]. 1966.
"Medan dagen svalnar" [As day grows cool]. In *Svenska radiopjäser 1968*. Stockholm: Sveriges Radios Förlag, 1968. Pp. 61–79.
"*Men vad ska dom säga på jobbet imorgon?*" [But what will they say at work tomorrow?]. 1967.
"Min farsa hade också en pokal" [My dad also had a silver cup]. In *Svenska radiopjäser 1971*. Stockholm: Sveriges Radios Förlag, 1971. Pp. 7–29.
Och sanningen skall göra eder fria [And the truth shall make you free]. 1981.
"Smultrontrollet" [The Wild Strawberry Troll]. In *Svenska radiopjäser 1967*. Stockholm: Sveriges Radios Förlag, 1967. Pp. 31–58.
Solkatten [Dazzled]. 1981.
"Stäng fönstret, morsan fryser!" [Shut the window, Ma's feeling cold!]. 1967.
"Överraskningen" [The surprise]. 1966.

5. Miscellaneous

Anteckningar från ett obekvämt privatliv [Notes from an Uncomfortable Private Life]. Bollnäs: Printed by Nyströms Boktryckeri for limited private distribution, 1976. Contains "När ångesten" and five short pieces, some of which had previously appeared elswhere.

"Brev hem" [Letter home]. *Frihet*, no. 7 (1959), pp. 24–25, 29.

Ensam på vinden med Pelle Kohlberg. En liten minnesbok [Alone in the attic with Pelle Kohlberg. A reminiscence]. Stockholm: Bonniers, 1981. Limited edition for distribution to Bonnier's friends and associates.

"Fusket" [Cheating]. In *Svenska noveller i TV* [Swedish short stories on television]. Stockholm: Sveriges Radios Förlag, 1978. Pp. 51–78.

"Jag har det bäst som jag har det" [I'm best off the way things are]. *Bonniers Litterära Magasin*, no. 3 (1972), pp. 120–26.

"Lidit har jag mycket sedan vi gick åtskils" [Great has been my grief since we parted]. *Femina*, no. 3 (1974), pp. 28–29.

"Mitt porträtt ar mig" [My portrait of myself]. *Vi*, no. 6 (1976), pp. 10–11. Evander's contribution to a series of authorial self-portraits in *Vi*.

"När ångesten" [When nameless fear]. *Bonniers Litterära Magasin*, no. 3 (1976). pp. 134–35. Poem.

"Prosadikter" [Prose poems]. *Svenska Dagbladet*, 21 December 1969.

"Sonen" [The Son]. *Bonniers Litterära Magasin*, no. 4 (1965), pp. 253–55.

"Tre minnen" [Three recollections]. *Fönstret*, no. 8 (1970), pp. 14–15.

6. Television productions (a selection)

Att leva är att ana [To live is to sense]. 1972.

Den blodiga kusten [The blood-stained coast]. 1975.

Den ynkryggen Valdemar [That poor wretch Waldemar]. 1980.

Det var ett kök med många bilder [There was a kitchen with many photographs]. 1969.

En gång i livet [Once in a lifetime]. 1969.

En högmodsdröm [Pride's dream]. 1971.

Fusket [Cheating]. 1978.

I morgon är en dröm [Tomorrow is a dream]. 1979.

I Puerto hände mig ingenting särskilt [Nothing special happened to me in Puerto]. 1971.

Mina hundar valde mig [My dogs chose me]. 1972.

Per Nilsson var mitt namn [Per Nilsson was my name]. 1972.

Plötsligt medan Harry levde [Suddenly, while Harry was alive]. 1971.

Resan från Främlingshem [The Journey from Strangers Haven]. 1972.

Till Josef med ömhet och ängslan [For Joseph—with love and anxiety]. 1972.

SECONDARY SOURCES

Ångesten kom klockan fem [Fear came at five o'clock]. 1972.
Återkomsten [The Return]. 1976.

Andersson, B. O. " 'Omgivningens grymma majoritet'—Ett centralt tema hos Per Gunnar Evander" ["The cruel majority of other people"—A central motif of Per Gunnar Evander's]. *Studiekamraten*, no. 7 (1967). pp. 124–126. About the first two novels and the early radio plays.

Bergsten, Anders. "Skuld och försoning—en studie i Per Gunnar Evanders författarskap" [Guilt and reconciliation—A study of the work of Per Gunnar Evander]. *Studiekamraten*, nos. 4–5 (1976), pp. 73–75.

Björkstén, Ingmar. "Vet mycket om ångest" [Knows a lot about fear]. *Svenska Dagbladet*, 31 July 1977. In the series "I helfigur" [Full-length portraits]. Pleasant introductory article.

Brandell, Gunnar, and Stenkvist, Jan. *Svensk litteratur 1870–1970*. Vol. 3. *Den nyaste litteraturen*. Stockholm: Aldus, 1975. Provides general background to modern Swedish literature and short presentation (pp. 151–53) of Evander's work.

Brostrøm, Torben. *Modern svensk litteratur 1940–1972*. Stockholm: Aldus 1973. Good background and brief presentation of Evander.

Edam, Anita. "Per Gunnar Evander, författare: Han skildrar de socialt förnedrade" [Per Gunnar Evander, author: He describes the socially humiliated]. *Fönstret*, no. 8 (1970), pp. 11–15. Evander's views on what a writer can do for society's weaker members.

Furenhed, Lennart. "Per Gunnar Evander lär oss att se och känna" [Per Gunnar Evander teaches us to see and feel]. *Kristet Forum*, no. 3 (1978), pp. 5–10. How the loneliness and lack of emotional contact of Evander's characters is gradually replaced by confidence.

Gustafsson, Lars. *The public dialogue in Sweden : Current issues of social, esthetic and moral debate*. Stockholm: Norstedts, 1964. Background to Evander's formative years prior to first novel.

Hedlund, Tom. *Mitt i 70-talet: 15 yngre svenska författare presenteras* [Halfway through the 1970s: A presentation of 15 young Swedish writers]. Stockholm: Forum, 1975. Pp. 46–69 on Evander. Excellent introduction.

Lagerlöf, Karl Erik. "Per Gunnar Evander erövrar kärleken" [Per Gunnar Evander captures love]. In *Strömkantringens år och andra essäer om den nya litteraturen*. Stockholm: Pan, 1975. Pp. 75–79. Appreciative essay on guilt and reconciliation in the novels from 1971 to 1973. The title essay *Strömkantringens år* [The watershed year] provides valuable insights into the politicization of Swedish literature around 1967.

Lindholm, Karl-Axel. "Per Gunnar Evander och fadersrollen" [Per Gunnar

Evander and the father figure]. *Horisont* no. 4 (1980), pp. 30–48. An attempt to trace the father figure as it appears in Evander's fiction.

Nettervik, Ingrid. "Per Gunnar Evanders skiftande ansikten" [Per Gunnar Evander's changing faces]. *Svensk litteraturtidskrift,* no. 2 (1980), pp. 26–31. Taking *Look Me in My Unblemished Eye* as starting point, the author provides a rapid survey of themes common to many Evander novels.

―――. "Per Gunnar Evanders roman 'Se mig i mitt friska öga' sedd mott bakgrunden av hans övriga författarskap" [Per Gunnar Evander's novel *Look Me in My Unblemished Eye* seen against the background of his work as a whole]. *Svensklärarföreningens årsskrift* 1980, pp. 32-50. Inventory of themes, situations, narrative technique, etc., intended for high school literature teachers.

―――. "Samhällskritik i Per Gunnar Evanders författarskap" [Social criticism in the novels of Per Gunnar Evander]. *Artes,* no. 6 (1980) pp. 100–08. Straightforward inventory.

New Swedish Books. Selected and presented by Bengt Erik Hedin, Kjell Sundberg, Lars-Olof Franzén, and Lennart Frick. Stockholm: Swedish Institute, 1974–79. Short presentations of new fiction, including Evander's.

Nilsson, Björn. "Per Gunnar Evander—en av de bästa författarna här i landet" [Per Gunnar Evander—one of the best writers in this country]. *Böckernas värld,* no. 4 (1971), pp. 90–96. Evander's work seen as "a sort of X ray of this society."

Petherick, Karin. "Inlevelsens logik. Per Gunnar Evander och författarrollen." [The logic of empathy. Per Gunnar Evander and the authorial role]. *BLM,* 3 (1981) pp. 139–146; Evander's creative method is seen as one of empathy, set against a climate favorable to objective analysis.

Rying, Matts. "Fredagarna med hr Evander" [Fridays with Mr Evander]. In *Ditt okända förflutna. En vänbok till Erik Hj. Linder,* edited by G. Helén, H. Linder and C. Ostberg. Stockholm: Natur & Kultur, 1976, pp. 179–95. Also published in Rying, *Tungomål: Samtal med diktare.* Stockholm: Rabén & Sjögren, 1979, pp. 192–206. Valuable interview touching on major aspects of Evander's work.

Index

(Works by Evander are listed under his name)